PSYCHOPATHS

JOHN CLARKE AND ANDY SHEA

PSYCHOPATHS

INSIDE THE MINDS OF THE WORLD'S MOST WICKED MEN

JOHN BLAKE

Published by John Blake Publishing Ltd,
3, Bramber Court, 2 Bramber Road,
London W14 9PB, England

www.blake.co.uk

First published in paperback in 2004

ISBN 1 84454 043 X

British Library Cataloguing-in-Publication Data:

A catalogue record for this book is available from the British Library.

Design by www.envydesign.co.uk

Printed in Great Britain by Bookmarque Limited, Croydon, Surrey

1 3 5 7 9 10 8 6 4 2

Papers used by John Blake Publishing are natural, recyclable products made
from wood grown in sustainable forests. The manufacturing processes conform to the
environmental regulations of the country of origin.

Every attempt has been made to contact the relevant copyright-holders, but some were
unobtainable. We would be grateful if the appropriate people could contact us.

All of that which is written and referred to in *Psychopaths* is based on fact. However,
in order to protect the identities of those individuals interviewed by the authors in
compiling this book, certain elements of the text, including the real identities and locations
of interviewees, have been changed. Any resemblance to real persons, either living
or dead, as a result of the changes, is purely coincidental.

'Note from John Clarke' is unedited as requested by its author.

To the victims

Contents

Acknowledgments

For my family, who have made me the person I am today through their selfless, unconditional love. And for B, who showed me the way.

JOHN CLARKE

Many people have helped make this book a reality and touched my life in the process. First and foremost amongst them are the individuals who have been the victims of psychopaths that I have interviewed and got to know personally. Many of whom have had their names changed in this book in order to protect their true identities. Without exception, I have found these people to be courageous and inspirational and I thank them for sharing with me their most painful moments. Prominent amongst them were Grace and Garry Lynch, the parents of Anita Cobby, whose spirit and outlook on life is nothing short of extraordinary. At the New South Wales Police Service, Paul Jacob, Rob Critchlow, Peter Whalan and Stewart Leggat deserve a special note of thanks for their time and patience in allowing me to tap into their wealth of experience in dealing with the kind of people nightmares are made of. Emma Ogilvie at the Australian Institute of Criminology was a godsend when it came to delving into the mind of the stalker, and Sunil De Silva at the New South Wales Directorate of Public Prosecutions was likewise extremely valuable when it came to assessing the impacts of fraudsters in Australia. Special mention must be made of Denise Brailey of RECA in Western Australia. A lot will be written of this crusading woman in the future, I am sure, but let me be the first to go on record as saying that she is a true and very real Australian hero of whom we should all be proud. Alex Faraguna at the Homicide Victims Support Group (NSW) was both helpful and informative above and beyond the call of duty from our very first meeting and without her I would never have been able to fully comprehend what it is like to survive the impact of a psychopath. In Canada, Dr Robert D. Hare proved more than worthy of his reputation as the world's leading expert on psychopathy and I am delighted that someone of his international standing could be so encouraging and spend the time to help me paint a realistic picture of the psychopath.

The team at Simon & Schuster Australia deserve a very special thanks for their support, guidance, belief and enthusiasm throughout the project. The redoubtable duo of Jody Lee and Bridget Howard, have been nothing short of superb, and together with our agent, Selwa Anthony, have turned a dream into reality. Without you it wouldn't have happened. Thanks.

Last, but by no means least, I would like to say a big thank you to my partner, Emma. My artistic pretentions have for the most part been unbearable and my lack of patience a definite bane during the writing of this book. The late nights and long writing weekends often took their toll, but through it all she has been there with a smile and words of wisdom, and a love that I know I am very, very lucky to have.

ANDY SHEA

Foreword

It was a Tuesday morning, I think, early anyway, when I came into contact with my first psychopath. I was working an early shift at the police station I worked at in Bethnal Green, a busy East London suburb, and had just booked on for duty. I was a probationary constable, barely out of training school. It was winter, cold and dark, and to be very honest, I was scared.

The night before a young Nigerian, who was working as a security guard on a local building site, had come into the station while I was on front desk duty. I was shocked at what I saw. The man's jaw and nose were obviously broken. His right eye was swollen as large as an orange. There was blood on his shirt, and cuts and welts on his face. He stood before me, crying, tears rolling down his face, and held out his left hand. Three bloodied teeth sat in the centre of his palm. He placed them on the counter before me, and then collapsed on the floor.

The security guard had been battered by a local hoodlum with a criminal record that boasted sexual assualt, grievous bodily harm, attempted murder, armed robbery and petty theft going back 15 years. This man lived on a local housing trust estate with his wife and two children. The reason for the beating and the terrible injuries I've just related was this: seeing two children clambering up the outside of some scaffolding, the security guard had shouted at them to come down as it wasn't safe and they were in danger of hurting themselves. The boys ignored him. Twice more the young Nigerian shouted at them. Twice more they ignored him. An hour later the boys began to throw sticks at the security guard as he walked on his patrol route. He told them to behave and chased them off the site. Ten minutes later the guard was approached by a large set man who punched him repeatedly in the face, and while hurling racial abuse at him, kicked and beat him about the head, chest and back until the Nigerian fell unconscious. Tragically, the Nigerian died four days later of massive brain injuries as a result of the beating he received.

I arrested the assailant on that cold Tuesday morning. Before I'd arrived at his house, I'd checked out his arrest record and had a look at his personal stats. He stood 6′9″ tall, weighed well over 16 stone with not an ounce of fat on him. When I saw him in person, his sheer size overwhelmed me. His hands were bigger than my head! My eyes were level with his belly button. He was a giant, and an angry one at that, seeing as it had only just turned 6 am when I awoke him to tell him he was under arrest for suspected assault. To say he came quietly to the station is an understatement, but that's an entirely different story!

This incident had a profound effect on me. Aspects of it have stuck in my mind ever since. Not just the injuries the victim received. Not just the sheer physical presence of the offender and the struggle to arrest him that followed that early morning knock on the door. Rather, the offender's complete and utter lack of emotion and reason for doing what he did, coupled with his almost dead, jet-black eyes, are the memories that have remained indelibly etched in my mind to this day. I interviewed the suspect at length with a couple of detectives following his arrest, and prior to him being charged with murder. I recall him as being cool, calm and without worry throughout. I remember thinking that he believed he was right and justified in doing what he did and being completely mystified by it. He is certainly one of the coldest and possible most vicious men I have ever met.

I went home that afternoon and began to think about what makes someone like that man tick? What is it that makes people like him so different from the vast majority of the population? What makes one person good, and another bad? What makes someone intentionally hurt or even worse, kill, another human being? What goes on in their minds? Why can't we stop them?

Since then I have been looking for answers and I've found many but not enough. I've read scores of books on psychopathy, the fundamentals of good and evil, serial killers, offender profiling and countless hundreds of other books on true crime. I've devoured all that can be read on killers such as Gacy, Bundy, Dahmer, Glover, Milat and Sutcliffe. I've read the minds of psychopaths through the excellent books of ex-FBI profilers and serial killer experts John Douglas and Robert Ressler, as well as those of social commentator Brian Masters and leading British psychologist Paul Britton. I've even sat down and developed my very own fictional monster in my first novel, *The Disciples*, in a bid to truly discover what it is like to be Touched by the Devil, and understand how psychopaths think and view the world around them.

I am constantly working on ideas and plots for my novels. I leave nothing to chance. Everything you read in one of my books is plausible, can be done, and in some cases, already has been done. There are people out there amongst you who are a whole lot worse than the killers I invent. I seek advice from experts, pathologists, cops, psychologists, profilers and even offenders, all with the aim of making my novels as believable as possible. This was how I met John Clarke.

I signed up to attend a course on serial killers given by John at Sydney University. After the lecture the two of us chatted over a coffee and I ran some ideas by him for characters in a couple of books I was then working on. I had long had an idea about writing a book on Australian psychopaths, detailing their minds, crimes and lives and how we very often live with them and don't know it until it's too late. As I talked to John, I sounded him out about the idea and told him what I wanted to do. I asked him if he would like to be involved in putting together such a book – him providing the psychological and developmental input and me writing and structuring it for a mainstream audience.

The result, less than a year later, is *Psychopaths*. It is a book that for the first time exposes the extent of the problem of psychopathy. It is a book that penetrates the minds of serial killers, rapists, stalkers, fraudsters and white-collar psychopaths. It is a book that tells for the first time the devastation caused by psychopaths on innocent people like you and me. It has provided me with even more answers as to why. I hope it does the same for you.

ANDY SHEA

INTRODUCTION

Behind the Mask

Psychopaths.

They intrigue and repulse, fascinate and frighten.

They are all around us, yet somehow hidden from our view. They are chameleons, these devils without conscience. They live apparently normal lives, for the most part doing normal things. Then one day, they change. Their world turns upside down and they embark on a destructive rampage that shakes our world, leaves blood on the streets, and shattered lives in their wake. And then, just as quickly as they appear, they vanish – until the next time.

Relentlessly single-minded in what they do, the terror of the psychopath is a constant threat to each and every person, 24-hours-a-day, every day of the year. They are out there now, perhaps sitting next to you, watching you read this, their eyes sweeping over you as you concentrate on these very pages. Or perhaps they are in a car around the corner from your house waiting for you to walk past on your way home. You may not know of their existence, but the psychopath knows of yours and is waiting and watching, biding his time until ready to attack. He or she may even be a colleague at work, or a friend you may be having dinner with tonight. They may even be someone you know intimately.

Welcome to the frightening world of the psychopath. A world that includes serial killers, rapists, stalkers and fraudsters. In this book we intend to take you on a journey into these individuals' minds. We will show you how they think, exposing along the way their innermost thoughts and fantasies. We will attempt to find reasons for why they commit their atrocious acts. We will illustrate the havoc and horror they cause. More importantly, we will tell you who these people are, how you can identify them and how you can avoid them and minimise your chances of becoming their next victim.

But before you can tackle the psychopath, you need to know who and what it is you are dealing with. You need to know your enemy. You need to know what makes them tick, what makes them do the terrible things they do.

Psychopaths are relentless. They stop at nothing to get what they want. They are driven by an obsessive need for power and control. They are an empty thing, devoid of any emotions or regret for what they do. They are almost inhuman in their ability to commit terribly selfish acts. And yet, while all this is true, in many ways the psychopath is just like you. He lives in the same world as you. He drives the same car. He rides the same bus and train. He reads the same newspapers, eats at the same restaurants, and does many of the things that you do. There is a touch of the psychopath in all of us. That is why we are so fascinated by them.

Psychopathy is a personality disorder or mental condition that can be defined by a distinctive cluster of psychological and behavioural traits or characteristics. Many of us possess these characteristics, yet not all of us can be considered psychopathic. What sets psychopaths apart from us is their utter lack of emotion – put simply they care about nothing.

Dr Robert D. Hare, PhD, is considered one of the world's leading authorities on psychopaths. Working from the University of British Columbia in Canada, Dr Hare and a number of his students have devised the Hare Psychopathy Checklist. This highly sophisticated and complex clinical tool has since become a worldwide standard used by researchers and clinicians to help them distinguish with reasonable certainty true psychopaths.

'The Checklist is a symptom rating scale designed to assess psychopathic and antisocial personality disorders,' says Dr Hare. 'It provides complete coverage of the range of psychopathic traits and behaviours.'

These traits cover three broad areas – interpersonal, emotional and behavioural characteristics. Interpersonally, the psychopath is grandiose, egocentric and manipulative, dominant and forceful. Emotionally, they display shallow emotions, which are highly changeable depending upon the circumstance. They are unable to form long lasting bonds with other people (though they can pretend a deep bond does exist), they have few if any principles or goals, and they have no empathy, nor do they feel anxiety or genuine guilt and remorse. In a behavioural sense, the psychopath is an impulsive and sensation seeking individual who readily violates socially acceptable norms though not always in an obvious manner.

To enable you to travel inside the psychopath's mind, so that you can truly understand what you are up against, we will highlight some of these traits here. However, it must be noted that the Hare Psychopathy Checklist is a complex clinical instrument that should only be administered by a trained professional. Because of this, we will only be providing a general description of the traits and characteristics commonly found in the psychopath, and *this summary should not be used to diagnose either yourself or anybody else as a psychopath. If you suspect anyone of being a psychopath, it is crucial that you obtain an expert opinion.*

It is equally important to realise that psychopathy is a complex cluster of these symptoms, as opposed to the presence of just a couple of them. In fact the checklist works by measuring the degree of each of the symptoms outlined for a particular person, and then assessing the totality of the symptoms in a person's lifestyle before making any diagnosis of psychopathy. Thus if you or someone you know has one or even a number of these symptoms, it does not necessarily imply the presence of psychopathy. Many people may be glib or cold or lack long-term goals. It doesn't necessarily mean they are psychopaths.

Emotional and interpersonal factors help characterise the psychopath's approach to life. These factors are the nucleus of their very reasoning processes – the things that shape their behaviour and mental abilities, indeed their very thoughts about their world. They are all vital facets of the psychopath's lethal repertoire and play a significant role in allowing them to capture their prey. They allow the psychopath to remain emotionless at the time of the attack. They allow him or her to disassociate themselves from social norms, enabling them to become ruthless, self-centred and conscienceless human predators.

The first of these factors is a glib and superficial charm. Generally, the psychopath is intelligent, and is perceived as very smooth and sophisticated. They are often the centre of attention. They possess excellent verbal skills and have a sharp mind that allows them to come across as charming and highly likeable. They are master storytellers, quick witted and very often weave a web of intrigue about how fantastic or wonderful they are.

Psychopaths are extremely effective at manufacturing an air of intellectual superiority. They may have a superficial under-standing of a wide range of topics, issues and professions, such as the media, science, law, medicine, politics, the environment and the arts. This knowledge will have been garnered by simply listening to other people conversing about these topics. The psychopath knows that by inserting the odd line or two into conversation, the person who is talking will continue, all the while educating the psychopath about the topic. Later, the psychopath will use this knowledge as part of a con or ruse to trap a potential victim.

Pulling something like this off is very easy for the psychopath. They are highly adept and expert liars with good memories. They also lack a conscience and feel neither guilt nor embarrassment when they are eventually caught lying and act as if nothing untoward has happened.

These individuals are excellent at creating the myth or illusion they believe their listener wants to hear, and they are equally good at recognising what 'buttons to push' for different people. An example of this comes from a psychopath we have dealt with in the course of writing this book. In an interview with him, the man, who we will call Kelvin, said this about what he wants from life:

> All I want in life to be happy is to be loved by someone, to find my soul mate. I want to share all of myself with this person. I feel like I am not complete yet, like I am only a half of a whole. Like I want to have meaning in my life and give some meaning to someone else's life.

Kelvin had recently split up from his wife. She had left the family home, citing his controlling nature as the reason for the split. Kelvin and his wife had a dog, a kelpie named Buck. Kelvin's wife loved Buck and wanted to take him with her, but couldn't manage to carry him when she left the house. She had intended to return the next day to collect him, but as it turned out didn't have to.

Kelvin had never liked the dog, but he knew that his wife loved him. Deciding to send her a message, Kelvin drove Buck to his wife's parent's home (where she had fled) and nailed the dog to the front door of the residence.

If you met Kelvin in a bar, or on the street, or even in his office, and he told you about his views on love and what he wanted from his life, you would feel you had met a decent and emotional human being. You would not for a moment suspect that he was the type of man who would nail a dog to his former soul mate's front door simply to send her a message.

A narcissistic and grandiose sense of self-worth is the next defin-ing characteristic of a person like Kelvin. The psychopath is always self-centred – in their own mind they are the most important person in the universe. These people possess an incredible sense of entitlement – they believe that they are entitled to have whatever it is they want to have and that it doesn't matter how they obtain it as long as they do.

They are the epitome of self-belief. For the psychopath, nothing in life is ever their fault – they are blameless. If something goes wrong or awry for them, or they fail at something, it is the system or society that is at fault or just a matter of bad luck. It is never they who are wrong. In fact, they believe that their abilities and intelligence allow them to achieve anything. They don't realise that they are greatly overestimating what they can and cannot do.

They are the centre of their world and they view other people as mere accessories or vehicles that they can use whenever they desire to get what they want. Dr Hare describes them as appearing 'charismatic or electrifying'.

'And for the most part they are,' he says.

We have been asked many times whether the psychopath feels remorse or guilt for any of their actions. The answer we give is always the same – no, they do not. However, this is not to say that they fail to realise that they have caused an incredible amount of suffering and distress as a result of what they have done. They do acknowledge the consequences of their actions. Rather, the reason for their lack of remorse and guilt is the fact that they are conscienceless – they do not care about people suffering, they feel nothing and many times cannot understand why other people would feel something.

As a result of this lack of human emotion, the psychopath has a certain amount of psychological freedom. For the majority of people, conscience prevents them from stealing or conning people, yet for the psychopath there is no such obstacle. All they are concerned about is the logistics of their crime, ensuring that nothing prevents it from going off smoothly and successfully. They may well pretend to feel bad about what they do or have done, but in reality they feel nothing. The only thing they regret is getting caught.

The psychopath will also look for excuses in order to rationalise his or her behaviour. A woman is raped because of the way she was dressed, people are defrauded because they are stupid, and anyway, they get all their money back from insurance companies, so what do they have to worry about? If these excuses fail to elicit the desired response, then the psychopath will try a different tack. He or she will claim that an illness that they have no control over was responsible for making them commit their crimes. We hear post-traumatic stress disorder, blackouts, temporary insanity and multiple personality disorder all cited as being the reasons for their evil. The psychopath will do whatever it takes for them to escape responsibility for their actions and minimise the punishment given to them.

Does the psychopath feel what other people feel? Can he feel their grief or terror? Does he have the capacity to empathise with others? The answers, once again, are no. Intellectually, the psychopath is able to conceptualise what other people are experiencing, but he or she has no ability whatsoever to truly know what it is like to be that other person and feel what they are experiencing.

Dr Hare even goes so far as saying, 'They lack qualities that are essentially needed to classify someone as human. The psychopath resembles the emotionless androids we often see depicted in science fiction.'

Their views on life are equally insensitive. In fact, they see life as merely the survival of the fittest in a harsh world. Psychopathic individuals we have dealt with believe that surviving in the world today is hard enough in itself without having to concern themselves too much about the way everyone else is feeling. This lack of concern, or empathy, is shown even to their closest family members.

A number of months ago we dealt with a woman, a single mother, who had dropped her two-year-old daughter in the middle of a busy street because she was crying. Her reason? Because her then boyfriend didn't like the noise. The child was taken into care. The mother told us she was angry and upset by this – not at what she had done, but because she felt that the social services had no right to take her daughter from her, and she was worried that people would think she was a bad mother because her only child had been taken from her. She then went on to say that it was entirely up to her how she disciplined her child and that no one had a right to tell her otherwise.

This is not a one-off case. Every day children are abandoned by their parents, many of whom would certainly fit the clinical definition of psychopathy. It is a terribly sad fact that this happens so often and it is something that we should all be concerned about.

The next characteristic assessed by the Hare Psychopathy Checklist is the deceitful and manipulative nature of the individual. The psychopath is an excellent liar, often pathologically so, and is able to lie with no apparent effort – almost, it seems, as easily as breathing. They are well versed at deceit and confuse their targets and the people they interact with by shifting from one topic to another so that whoever is listening finds it difficult to keep up with the flow of conversation. If caught lying, the psychopath will not falter. Instead, he or she will create an elaborate explanation for their untruth or ignore the discovery and move on to a new subject in such a manner as to further confuse the listener.

Psychopaths are proud of their talent for lying – they feel it is further proof of their overwhelming intelligence. Whether it be constructing an elaborate ruse to get a woman into their car in order to rape and murder her, or defrauding a company or community of millions of dollars, the psychopath's level of deceit and verbal skills are almost unsurpassed.

The final emotional and interpersonal characteristic of the psychopath is that of shallow emotion. They are cold-blooded and ruthless. They associate love with sexual arousal, anger with irritability. They also display very little fear. We know this from psychophysiological research that has been conducted on a large number of convicted psychopaths. This is an important issue to consider when trying to understand how the psychopath's mind works. Fear is an inhibitor. The sense of fear prevents us from doing certain things. However, for the psychopath this thought process does not occur. They are not afraid of doing whatever it is they want to do.

Now that we know how these people think, to be able to fully understand them we also need to know how they function in terms of behaviour. The Hare Psychopathy Checklist helps us with this task too, by looking for signs of impulsiveness in a suspected individual's lifestyle.

The psychopath does not generally spend an extensive amount of time looking at the positives and negatives of their behaviour – quite often they will act on impulse, seeking the quickest means possible to instant excitement, pleasure, relief or satisfaction. This makes them very unpredictable.

The psychopath lacks self-control. As we have just seen, they are impulsive, possess no inhibitory mechanisms to prevent them from doing wrong and causing harm, and they are easily offended, even over the most trivial of things. The mere act of accidentally bumping into one of these individuals can be enough to start a torrent of verbal and often physical abuse.

Such seemingly innocuous actions are seen by the psychopath as challenges to his or her dominance and supremacy. Striking out at someone who offends them is a way in which the psychopath feels he or she can regain those feelings of power and control. To them, punching someone who has bumped into them and issuing a host of expletives is a totally justified reaction, and one that is necessary in this difficult world. In the psychopath's mind it is necessary to show they are not someone to be 'messed with'.

Psychopaths are easily bored and have an intense desire for excitement. They need to be stimulated and challenged constantly. Research has actually found that not only does the psychopath need continued excitement and stimulation, but that it takes more for a psychopath to be excited than it does for the average person. This means that where you or I may find driving a sports car, abseiling or skydiving exciting, the psychopath needs to be in a stolen sports car being chased by the police to experience the same level of excitement that we do. Similarly, where we experience pleasure and excitement from meeting people at work, the psychopath needs to play psychological games with these people and destroy them in order to feel the same level of excitement and satisfaction. Psychopaths live in a very different world indeed.

In no other crime is this need for perverse excitement so clearly shown as in that of a murder committed by a psychopathic serial killer. For the psychopath, sex is not gratifying enough. The serial killer needs more than this. His feelings of intense excitement come from terrorising and killing the victim, and watching them die before his eyes at the same time as he reaches an orgasmic climax. Despite this seemingly sexual element to the crime, it is vital to take into account that sex alone is not a motivating factor in any psychopath's behaviour, no matter what their crime. The psychopath is a person who because of his or her upbringing and biological make-up is without conscience. A psychopath has no regards for other people and is a purely selfish organism focused completely on satisfying his or her desires. This desire to satiate themselves is achieved in many ways, from sexual violence (for example rape) to psychologically destroying people in the workplace or killing people for money (for example, a hitman). Despite the ambiguous terminology, the sexually violent offender is not necessarily motivated by a desire for sex. Rather these terrifying individuals are driven by an unstoppable need for power and control and sexual violence is simply a weapon that is used to achieve this.

Knowing that a psychopath is easily bored and knows no fear, does this mean that they are suitable for high-risk jobs?

We agree with Dr Hare on this matter when we respond that no, they are not. These people may well be fearless and need ample doses of adrenaline, but they are also impulsive and have little or no self-control. In addition they are unstable and don't respond well to discipline. They will tend to look for employment in the services such as the army, navy and police or find work in the security industry – professions that allow an individual to experience a certain degree of power and control – but inevitably their careers will not last long. It is one reason we see many psychopaths that are professional career nomads, wandering from one job to the next, with no focus being placed on the importance of a stable career. However, our experience has shown that in many workplaces there is a person who could be considered psychopathic. It is a bold statement, but it is a true one, based solely on our research and experience. There are a large number of psychopaths who find work in the white-collar world – and succeed. We will discuss these white-collar psychopaths later, and look at how they manage to psychologically exercise power and control over their colleagues and senior managers on a daily basis. These white-collar psychopaths do stay in their jobs for as long as they are able, as these jobs provide them with a psychological 'killing field'. It is the criminal psychopath who tends to shift jobs repeatedly.

Childhood and adult antisocial traits are also assessed by the Checklist in a bid to give as clear a picture as possible as to what a psychopath is. We mentioned a little earlier that precursors to psychopathy are evident even in the early stages of these individuals' lives. Often we come into contact with a child who has a complete disregard for other people. They may well lie, cheat and steal. As they get older, they might be cruel to animals, deliberately start fires, destroy property, repeatedly skip school, and run away from home.

As they grow older and become an adult they may well have numerous impersonal sexual relationships. They will make their own rules for how they act and what they do. They will happily hurt people to get what they want. This doesn't necessarily mean that they will break the law. Far from it. Rather, they will be unethical in everything they do. They may cheat on their spouse, neglect their children or simply fail to live up to their promises. Whatever they do, they will cause hurt and heartache, and they will continue to act this way, increasing the extent of their deviant behaviour until it is too late.

Knowing this about the psychopath, you may be wondering why we are so fascinated and intrigued by such terrible and frightening individuals. Perhaps the reason we are so interested in them is because fundamentally they are very much like us. In fact, if we were honest, and thought for a moment about the characteristics and personality traits exhibited by these monsters, we would realise they are simply extreme versions of ourselves. Many of us are glib and just as many of us are self-important, but thankfully we are not all psychopaths.

We all live in the same world, and utilise the same mental processes in our daily lives. We drive the same cars, read the same newspapers and watch the same TV shows. All of us want to be loved. We are similar in so many ways, yet the majority of us do not go out of our way to terrorise, abuse and destroy people. It is not the sole purpose of our existence. We find satisfaction in different ways.

It is a complex chain of certain psychological and behavioural factors that differentiates psychopaths from the rest of us. There is no massive gulf between us. Perhaps this is why we are so fascinated by psychopaths.

Fortunately for society we are not all capable of being a devil in the real world. Our consciences prevent this from happening, as do our strategies and abilities to cope with events that happen to us both as children and adults.

You are now ready to begin your journey into the world of the psychopath. What you find along the way may disturb you. It may shock and appal you, but it is real. This is a glimpse into a part of society that surrounds you every day. Psychopaths live and work among us. We are all vulnerable to their threat. *Psychopaths* will help you avoid becoming a victim.

CHAPTER 1

On the Hunt

Like wild animals, psychopathic serial killers meticulously track their prey, watching their potential victim's every move, carefully planning the where and when of their attack, playing the fantasy over and over in their minds until it consumes their every waking moment.

They become completely focused on the task they have set themselves, retreating into their own fantasy world, enjoying the feelings of control it brings. Soon, they know, they will break away from society's rules and experience what is for them a divine moment and for others a moment of abhorrent horror. Their extraordinary desires drive them on. They look for the weakest and most vulnerable members of society – in most cases women. They watch and wait, all the while running through in their minds the approach, the attack, that all-encompassing moment when their hapless and innocent victim breathes their last painful breath.

This is how a serial killer thinks. How do we know? Because

they've said so, time and time again, in magazine interviews, books, films, documentaries, sometimes at court, and even moments before they are executed.

What goes on in the mind of a killer as he hunts down and eventually kills another human? Along with 'why?' this is perhaps the most intriguing question often asked of serial killers, and one which the killers themselves relish answering.

John Wayne Gacy, known as the Killer Clown (he would dress up as a grinning clown called Pogo and entertain hospitalised children when he wasn't enticing young boys and men to his house where he would later kill them), said that his encounters with victims were 'happenchance'. He didn't consciously go out looking for victims, he said shortly before his execution, he simply drove through areas where he thought he might find runaways. When he came across someone he liked, he would charm them and lead them to their deaths.

In an interview with ex-FBI agent Robert Ressler, Milwaukee serial killer Jeffrey Dahmer describes how he found one of his victims. 'I invited one guy I had met in front of gay bar back to the hotel just for a night of thrills and sex … he was a nice looking guy … We drank … he fell asleep, I continued drinking and I must have blacked out because I remember nothing before waking up in the morning. He was on his back, his head was over the edge of the bed, and my forearms were bruised and he had broken ribs and everything. Apparently I'd beaten him to death.'

David Berkowitz, otherwise known as the Son of Sam, shot dead six young New York men and women between 1976 and 1977. His weapon of choice was a .44 calibre revolver. After his arrest, Berkowitz had this to say about his bloody killing spree that had terrorised the city: 'I didn't want to hurt them. I only wanted to kill them. I feel like an outsider. I am on a different wavelength from everybody else. I am programmed to kill.'

Perhaps the most chilling words ever spoken by a convicted serial killer which describe the senselessness of such murders, are those words of Henry Lee Lucas, who is suspected by some investigators of killing as many as 69 people. At his 1985 trial, Lucas was convicted of 10 first-degree murders. Before his death in 2001, he had this to say: 'Killing someone is just like walking outdoors. If I wanted a victim, I'd just go and get one.'

The chilling fact is that psychopaths can now be found across the globe. Amongst the most infamous names are Jeffrey Dahmer, Ted Bundy and Hohn Wayne Gacy in America, John Wayne Glover, Ivan Milat and Edward Leonski in Australia and Peter Sutcliffe and Dennis Nilson in the UK, sadly the list goes on. Serial murder is becoming more common. Why this is so is hard to say, but criminologists admit that the number of homicides and serial sexual offenders is increasing.

While this may come as a terrifying shock to some people, what is even more shocking is the fact that there are a staggering number of individuals living and working amongst us who fantasise about killing someone. For many, these fantasies are kept locked away and the desire to kill is tempered by the possibility of being caught and handed a lengthy prison sentence. For some, this is enough of a deterrent to stop them from fulfilling their deviant fantasies.

However, for a small number of others, the lives they are

currently living are mere preludes to the mayhem they fully intend to accomplish at some time in the near future. The frightening fact is, that as you read this book and delve into the world of the psychopath, there are a number of people out there plotting murderous campaigns and counting the days until they fulfil their destiny. These are people living and working with us who want to kill. It is their ultimate desire. They want to feel what it's like to snuff out the life of a stranger. They want to embark on a controlled killing spree and feel they are clever and cunning enough to get away with it. How do we know this? Because we have met one.

Sam

People pass by him on the street and he watches them. Not the disinterested kind of people-watching and everyday curiosity that is par for the course in a large city on a busy day. For Sam this is all part of the game, his ritual. As he walks through a crowded street, or sitting at a café or bar glancing this way and that, he is people shopping, picking out the ones he likes, the ones he can fantasise about owning, controlling and destroying. The ones he would like to kill.

Sam is a handsome, fit man of 28, standing almost two metres tall, with the kind of body you'd expect to find on someone who spends a lot of time in the gym and eats nothing but fish and steamed vegetables. He has no problems in attracting members of the opposite sex, and has the looks and charm that could convince even the most severe and cynical of would-be mother-in-law's that he's a good catch.

Sam was born and raised in the same city, and has lived there most of his life, except for a short time when he was sent away to live with his father's family abroad. It is a period of his life that he doesn't want to talk about and is determined for whatever reason to forget. Despite a somewhat turbulent childhood, Sam performed well enough at school to pass his exams and gain a college place studying graphic design. For the past year he has been working for a small design and advertising agency. He doesn't like his job and can't stand the people he works with, but feels it will have to do for now. He lives alone in a rented apartment on the outskirts of the city and drives a nondescript Volkswagen Golf GL.

Sam has recently broken up with his girlfriend, Jayne. He is coy about why the relationship broke down, but is adamant that it wasn't his fault and that she was to blame for everything that went on. She is a liability, he says. She knows too much. Her time will come. Listening to him say these words and sensing the feelings contained within them, you know he means it.

Sam doesn't like to talk about the past, about his father or about Jayne either for that matter. For Sam the past is a painful and agonising memory. This past is full of loud, screaming voices, fighting parents and extreme pain. The past, he says, is best forgotten. He is over it. The future is his only concern. It is a future he is systematically moulding and preparing himself for and could well lead to unbearable heartache.

'There's so many of them,' Sam told us. 'So many people out there. Just waiting, waiting for the end. I feel this is what I am here for.'

Sam can't remember where his urges to kill came from, but

he will tell you quite openly that they are there and that he doesn't know how long he can control them. He claims he is frightened at times by the thoughts in his mind. Whether this is true, or is simply his way of excusing himself for what he feels, is difficult to say, but Sam's childhood and his early adult life hold some clues as to the way in which he has developed into the frightening person he is today.

He says that he woke up one day when he was a child and felt like he had changed – like his destiny had been shaped somehow, by a power he couldn't fully comprehend. Since then, he has been on a seemingly relentless pursuit of blood, which has every chance of becoming a tragedy for someone, somewhere, soon. There are no voices inside his head driving him on, he states. No voices. Just his mind, telling him where his destiny lies and how he should go about fulfilling it.

It is uncommon for serial killers to believe that they are possessed by a satanic force or spirit. Often this excuse is used after the offences have been committed and the killer has been captured. It is used as an excuse by the killer to exonerate himself legally and psychologically from the burden of having committed the acts. In reality, it isn't the devil that makes a serial killer murder his victims. Rather it is a conscious decision that enables him to experience the lust for power and control that is expressed through a perverse and deviant sexual act culminating in the death of another person.

Sam is the third child of his father and the second child of his mother, both immigrants who arrived seeking a new life in the late 1950s. His family background can at best be described as dysfunctional. The only male member of the family (apart from his father), Sam often felt neglected and unloved as a child and constantly lived in the shadow of his sisters and half-sister, who he claims were worshipped by his now dead mother – a woman he still despises with a blazing fury and blames for destroying his life.

His parent's marriage was a troubled one. With no friends or family to support them in their new homeland and money often tight, arguments – almost always violent – were an everyday part of life for the young Sam.

'My parents fought day and night,' he says. 'The fights were loud, with lots of swearing and screaming. Things would be smashed and punches would be thrown. It wasn't a peaceful or happy time. I hated them both. I'm glad that they're both dead now. It's a relief.'

Sam's father was an alcoholic with a violent temper. Working as a barman in a local pub, he would come home every night heavily intoxicated and beat his wife in full view of the children. He would then turn his attention and his fists to his son.

'He'd beat me,' says Sam. 'Kick and punch me until all I could do was roll up into a ball, close my eyes and wish for it to stop.'

The parental abuse Sam describes is one of the most important formative events in many sexual homicide offenders' development. Studies conducted on serial killers have revealed that in 75 per cent of cases, the killer has experienced some form of abuse as a child.

Three types of abuse are important in the context of the formation of the serial killer – physical abuse, sexual abuse and psychological abuse. Each of these forms of abuse shatters the person's feeling of control over their own life. As a child Sam would have felt that no matter what he did, he could not escape the physical and psychological abuse he was experiencing at the hands of his father. The only avenue of escape available to Sam, was a retreat into a fantasy world.

This fantasy world would be dominated by thoughts of gaining complete control over everything in his life, as a reaction to his perception of having no control in reality. Complete control over other people, owning them, as it were, in a desperate attempt to prevent his fragile identity from disintegrating.

The deviant parental modelling illustrated by Sam's parents is another critical factor we can see clearly illustrated in this case. Children generally learn at a young age what is appropriate behaviour from their parents in the socialisation process. Essentially we are all products of a combination of our genetic inheritance and upbringing. As a child, alone in his fantasy world, Sam's learning and development process was turned upside down. Early on he discovered a number of strategies he has since employed throughout his life. He learnt that control stems from physical violence toward other people. Using his father as his role model, he learnt how to instil psychological terror. He also discovered that it is possible to escape from a feeling of complete powerlessness by fantasising about controlling other people. More importantly, Sam learnt that in this world only the fittest survive. Therefore, if Sam wants something, whether that something be power and control, a car, a woman or money, the only person he can rely on to get it is himself.

He has learnt that there are no negative consequences for controlling other people – after all, his parents were never punished for this, so, as far as he's concerned, it must be right. In fact, Sam has learnt that controlling other people is rewarding and feels incredibly gratifying. This has reinforced his behaviour and has set him up for a lifetime of seeking to manipulate, dominate and control other people. Over the years he has learnt not to feel any emotion for the plight of others, and, by his own admission, has sometimes experienced an almost ecstatic feeling in the face of other people's suffering and terror. This is what makes Sam feel in control. It has confirmed in his mind that he holds all of the power in life.

In people like Sam, this deviant cognitive coping style (or thought process) reinforces itself throughout their lives, as they interpret everything in a manner that justifies their constant quest for power and control. What they fail to realise, however, is that by thinking this way, they are doomed to a life of emptiness, as they are seeking control over themselves by attempting to control other people. Unlike the rest of us, they don't understand that they can only ever have control over their own lives by searching deeply within themselves, as opposed to destroying other people.

The poor parenting models and abuse certainly play a major role in both the formation and maintenance of this problematic thought process. It is one of a number of essential steps in the formation of the psychopath.

While physical abuse was dished out to Sam by his father, emotional and psychological abuse came from his mother who Sam says hated him because he looked like his father and reminded her of him.

'I would do something wrong and she would rant at me that I

was a piece of shit, like my father, that I was good for nothing scum, that I was "just like him",' Sam reveals.

Despite an above-average report card from school and a prowess for sports, Sam's progress was never apparently good enough for his demanding parents and as the child became a teenager, he quickly began to trust no one but himself and became a loner, with few friends.

More worryingly, he became fascinated with animals, and in particular the trust he could inspire in them with a soothing and calm voice, and the hurt and pain he could cause them when he had them under his control.

'Animals are nothing because they can't talk,' he says, explaining his apathy towards them. 'I don't care about them, I can't understand why people get so upset when their dog or cat dies. It's just a fucking animal, nothing more.'

From the age of about 13, Sam began to find pleasure in torturing, killing, dissecting and burying animals of all types. He would spend hours trawling the streets around his home looking for road-kill – animals that had been killed by vehicles on the local roads and left in the gutter. When he found a carcass, he would take it to a nearby park, where he felt comfortable and safe from prying eyes, and hack into it using a pocket-knife that he'd stolen from a local hardware shop. Here he would revel in what he was doing and enjoy for the first time an intense sexual thrill at the sight of the dead animal's internal organs and its blood on his hands.

This was a pivotal moment for Sam. Alone and lost in a world of his own creation, he could exert power and control over something that couldn't fight back. At the same time, he'd experience the kind of intense sexual pleasure his frequent bouts of masturbation with stolen pornographic magazines never brought him.

After a few months, Sam had moved from picking up dead animals to hunting for them himself – catching birds, cats, possums, lizards and frogs to perform what he calls 'experiments' on them. One such experiment involved tying the legs of a cat together then placing it in the middle of City Road, one of Sydney's busiest main streets. Hobbled and howling, the cat was hit by three cars as it tried desperately to avoid the rush of the oncoming traffic and survive. Sam watched it all, with a growing erection, from the safety of a nearby bridge. On another day, Sam visited his sister's house to look after her two children for the morning. He'd been looking forward to the babysitting duty for weeks, he recalls, not because it was an opportunity to see his young nephews, but because it would give him a chance to play with his sister's pet birds – a cockatiel and a macaw.

Within an hour of his sister leaving the house, both birds were dead – their necks broken by Sam as the children watched and played on the floor. He says that when his sister returned and saw that the birds were lying dead on the floor, she tried to stab him. He punched her in the face, calling her a 'slut' as he did so, then ran out of the house laughing. He has not seen her since. That was six years ago.

Sam has drowned at least a dozen strays by tying bricks to their tails and legs and throwing them in a river.

This cycle of violence against animals had increased over the years. By the time he was 16, Sam had a 'pet cemetery' in his backyard that housed over 50 different dead and mutilated animals. His fascination with their inner workings and the sexual thrill he received from seeing the insides of an animal, has led him to experiment with sex using these internal organs, a behaviour he continues to practice today.

In the same way in which Sam has been fascinated by animals and the destruction he can cause them, fire has also played an important role in his life over the years. At the time he began to experiment with animals, Sam also began experimenting with fire. In fact, he says with a smile, his pet cemetery would have housed more specimens had he not cremated them. Over a series of six months, just prior to his nineteenth birthday, Sam claims to have started at least eight fires, including one at an abandoned farmhouse in rural Victoria.

The fascination with fire is a common characteristic observed in the majority of serial killers interviewed to date and many of them have at least two of three other characteristics from what is known as the 'homicidal triad'. The three factors that comprise the homicidal triad are a fascination with fire, or pyromania, cruelty to animals or other small children, and finally enuresis (bed wetting) after an inappropriate age (nine to ten years old).

The first two characteristics certainly indicate a need for asserting power and control over other people and their environment, in terms of both destruction of property and physical and psychological cruelty.

The lighting of a fire makes the person feel in complete control over everything. The sight of the flames devouring all in their path indicate to the child that they are capable of incredible destruction of physical things that are precious to other people. This is then linked to the destruction of people psychologically.

The fire brigade and police all attend the blaze, indicating to the child that they are important and are noticed by society, ensuring everyone recognises their power over life. This can lead to a feeling of excitement and control.

From this, fire starting is then linked in the offender's mind to sexual arousal and perhaps gratification from subsequent masturbation, reinforcing the act's potency. The sexual satisfaction then strengthens the pleasurable sensations experienced in the act of arson, leading to serial repetition of the behaviour. Quite often the serial arsonist will keep extensive logs or diary entries, detailing exact specifications of each fire set, as a trophy they can use to remember each fire. With this, they will relive their actions and derive extreme satisfaction from the memories, just as we derive satisfaction from looking at holiday photographs after the event.

Not all serial killers find arson a satisfactory channel for gratification of their needs for power, control and sexual arousal, however. It is for this reason that not all serial killers turn to serial arson, but certainly a number of them use it as one form of gratification from time to time.

Cruelty to animals and small children once again serves the need of showing the offender, who feels they have no control over any aspect of their life, that in fact they do have control over something – things weaker and more vulnerable than themselves. The experience of seeing another living object in pain serves to reinforce in their own minds how powerful they are. This torture makes them feel fantastic. They learn there are no consequences for being cruel to other living things, as their parents often do not punish them, as was the case with Sam.

They then learn that to feel in control over life they need to harm another living thing. As they develop into adolescents and then adults they discover more and more channels to express this cruelty, culminating in the torturous acts they commit on human victims they use to fulfil their desires.

Similarly to arson, the act of cruelty is associated with sexual gratification, particularly with the onset of puberty. This then leads to sexual forms of torture being expressed in the serial murderer's behavioural repertoire, who can be termed as a 'sexual homicide offender'.

The reason for the frequency of bed wetting in the development of serial killers remains a complete mystery.

A child who possesses all three of these characteristics will not necessarily become a serial killer, but it is certainly a sign for extreme concern and should be monitored closely. In researching this book, we have come across a number of cases of children with the homicidal triad living out in the community who are not being monitored or treated. Essentially they are time bombs waiting to explode with no one attempting to defuse them. In our lectures on serial murder we are frequently approached at the end of the developmental section by a parent who knows 'someone' with a child like the one we have just described. Quite often they then tell us nothing is being done for the child, as no one seems to be able to help them.

The elements of the homicidal triad expand as the child becomes an adolescent, into robbery, car theft, cruelty to animals, joyless, hostile aggressive play patterns, a disregard for others, destruction of property and sexual offences. As an adult they engage in behaviours including assault, burglary, arson, abduction, torture and rape, murder and mutilation. The progression from the homicidal triad to these types of behaviour is not yet fully understood, but certainly it appears that a clear link exists between immature expressions of the need for power, control and dominance, and the manifestation of these in a more mature and sinister form in adulthood.

In the case of Sam, we can clearly see the evidence of this progression, with the exception of bed wetting (or at least it was not reported) right through to the fantasising about the commission of a sexual homicide. Assaultive behaviours, theft and arson have all been committed, but the threshold to enter the next phase is yet to be crossed.

The past five years have seen Sam develop a fantasy where he abducts a lone female, takes her home and tortures her until she can stand no more. At the moment of her death Sam wants to 'devour her spirit'.

'At that moment,' he says, 'She will become one with me. I will own her.'

Almost every night, he sits at home and works through his plan. He runs through in his mind exactly how it will happen, what will be said and what will be done. More importantly for him, he imagines the extreme experience of control – the ultimate power – and the ability to give and take away life. This sense of power is inextricably linked to sexual satisfaction, which partially explains the repetition of, and obsession with, the behaviour.

Sam has countless diary entries dedicated to the scheme. Page after page detailing in painstaking and minute detail his plan of attack and fantasies. It is the diary of a sick man with a warped and twisted mind. He says that he wants to consume the soul of another human being. His dream is for the pain of death caused by him to be the last thing the victim is aware of.

He wants to eat the flesh of his victim, although he says quite candidly that he might not have the stomach for it. He wants to inflict pain and suffering on an individual for the sheer thrill of it, in an attempt to see just how much pain a person can take. He wants to be God. He wants to control. He wants to be the ultimate harbinger of death.

'One of my favourite quotes is from Ted Bundy,' Sam revealed to us. 'Ted talked about what it was like to be there at the final moment, the moment of death. He said, "You feel the last bit of breath leaving their body. You're looking into their eyes. A person in that situation is God." That's my aim. I want that experience to be mine.'

A number of theories exist attempting to explain how a person becomes a serial killer. Studies have been and are still being conducted by the FBI, law enforcement bodies around the world, psychologists, psychiatrists and academics. Each of these theories has certain common elements, but here we will attempt to provide a holistic account of the development of the serial killer. Elements of other models that appear relevant have been incorporated.

Essentially the serial killer requires two components in order to develop: the biological element and the environmental/psychological element of their behaviour. Both of these are necessary for the serial killer to evolve. This may explain why some people who grow up in abusive situations do not become serial killers – perhaps a different biological make-up prevents this from occurring.

Different coping strategies are used to deal with the stress of losing control. This could also explain why the vast majority of serial killers are male. Men have a different neurophysiological structure to women. This may well account for the disproportionate ratio of male to female psychopaths. However, the exact mechanisms that are thought to cause this propensity for violence in the male are not fully understood.

Fortunately for society, the combination necessary for a person to become a serial killer is reasonably rare per capita of population. However, in a large number of ways, the serial killer is similar to you. The vast majority of the time, they think about the same things you do. They appear to fit into society. They act the same as you. Like you, they desire pleasure.

The fundamental difference is the fact that they experience limited, if any, guilt, and they achieve gratification differently to most people. They are less inhibited in how they achieve pleasure, to the extent that they will kill other people to do so.

The FBI has put forward a comprehensive model of why and how individuals become serial killers, based upon studies carried out on serial homicide offenders throughout the United States. While the study's findings relate solely to North American killers, our research has shown that all serial killers display characteristics and personal histories similar to their US counterparts. However, a number of important additions need to be included in order to fully comprehend what it is like to be inside the mind of a serial killer and how they become what or who they are in the first place.

A question often asked by clinicians and scientists who devote their time to understanding psychopaths is whether their subjects are born or made. The most comprehensive explanation is that a unique combination of a number of biological abnormalities interact with the child's environmental experiences culminating in the formation of a serial killer or sexual offender.

Neurologists have recently found evidence that suggests that some people may have a predisposition to becoming psychopathic. They point to studies conducted on psychopaths in prison, which show that many of them suffer from malfunctions in the brain that could be the root of the problem. However, it is impossible for us to ever know if the psychopath was born with those biological abnormalities or whether the abnormalities are a result of environment. We believe it is a combination of the two.

These neurological abnormalities include a malfunctioning of the amygdala – the part of the brain that controls emotion. Abnormal pre-frontal cortex activity has also been found in psychopaths. The pre-frontal cortex is connected to the amygdala and is responsible for decision-making. In normal people, these parts of the brain have a very strong interaction with one another and enable us to learn and understand appropriate behaviour patterns. However, research carried out in Britain and the United States has revealed that the interaction between the amygdala and pre-frontal cortex in a psychopath's brain is very weak and could be the reason for the psychopath's utter lack of emotion and regret with regard to their actions.

There are other types of brain dysfunction that have been found in psychopaths. Positron Emission Tomography (PET) scanning, which produces a picture of the activity within different parts of the brain, has shown a disturbance in the temporal lobes of psychopaths. The temporal lobes, situated just above the ears, are responsible for our sense of self and, amongst other things, spirituality. Damage to this part of the brain, say scientists, may explain why psychopaths feel little sense of personal responsibility and an enormous sense of self-worth.

Scientists have also discovered that many serial killers have low levels of cortisol in their blood or saliva. Cortisol is a steroid hormone produced by the body in times of stress. People with low levels of arousal who are easily bored, such as psychopaths, have very low cortisol levels and rarely become stressed.

Serotonin levels are also low within psychopaths. Serotonin is one of the chemicals used by the brain for communications between nerve cells. In normal people it acts as a brake on brain cell activity. People with low levels of serotonin are often irritable and easily angered and in some instances have a sense of impulsiveness and lack of self-control.

While neurological malfunctions may well play a big part in making a psychopathic serial killer who he is, it is certainly clear that an ineffective social environment and upbringing is also critical in the formation of their personality and deviant approach to life.

One of a parent's most important functions is to guide their offspring along an appropriate path to function within the society in which they live. They set the tone for the child's behaviour and development from the moment that child is born. Showing the child that they are loved, needed, wanted and valued is crucial in this, as is demonstrating the difference between right and wrong and showing what is acceptable and non-acceptable behaviour.

It is common to observe severe deficiencies in each of these areas in the upbringing of the serial killer. Parents of would-be serial killers often ignore the behaviour of their child, providing no guidance or direction as to what is right or wrong. The child therefore never realises which behaviours are or are not appropriate. As a consequence they often do not believe that their inappropriate behaviour or actions are wrong, as they have never been told otherwise by the most significant adults in their lives, namely their parents. This non-intervention also results in the child not understanding that society has certain behavioural rules.

In addition, the child of abusive parents feels as though the only person they can rely upon is themselves. They believe the only person who can make them happy and fulfilled is themself. This leads to them feeling unwanted and undervalued by their parents and society. As a result they do not feel secure in life, both physically and psychologically, and as Sam's case has shown, these feelings fester over the years.

All of this evidence helps us to put ourselves inside the developing mind of a serial killer. Imagine for a moment that you are a child aged anywhere between five and eight years old. You do as you please on a daily basis, neither being punished nor rewarded for your actions. You feel that your parents do not care about you. They have no time for you, show you no affection or sympathy and treat you as if you are an unnecessary burden to them. How would you feel? What kind of person do you believe you would grow up to become?

While the vast majority of you would not grow up to become a serial killer, this is precisely the framework upon which a number of serial killers' psychological approaches to life evolve, although a plethora of more complex factors are included in the developmental mix.

Physical and sexual abuse is reported as being present in the developmental history of many serial sexual homicide offenders. Psychological abuse is even more commonly reported, with some offenders reporting all three forms of abuse.

Imagine again that you are the child mentioned earlier. Try to visualise the feelings and emotions of what it must be like to experience all of these factors at a time in your life when you are supposed to be carefree and able to trust everybody to help you grow and develop into an adult. Most importantly, imagine the immense feeling of absolute loss of control over every aspect of your life. No matter what you do, you simply cannot escape the physical violation of your body and the psychological damage resulting from these cruel acts.

You are completely powerless. You are at the mercy of someone who is physically and psychologically much stronger and more powerful than you. You are also learning that life is cruel and only the fittest survive. You are learning a host of more lethal lessons in life.

You desire a feeling of power and control, and the abuse you suffer leads you to believe that the sexual violation of another person can bring these feelings. You have just learnt a strategy for gaining control over another person in an attempt to gain a feeling of power and control over yourself and your destiny.

The fact that this abuse is being carried out by a close family member, who by rights should be protecting and nurturing you, causes you to feel as though you owe society and everybody else around you nothing. The only person you owe anything to in life is yourself. You feel that no one else will look out for you and you believe it fruitless to care for anybody else, to worry how they feel or be troubled by what happens to them. This is termed as possessing a negative social attachment, which could explain why some individuals appear to be so callous in dealing with other people in society.

Because of the fact that as that child you feel little to nothing emotionally and physically for other human beings, you display and feel diminished emotions when it comes to dealing with people. Another person's suffering for you is insignificant. As long as you are happy, nothing else matters.

A process known as desensitisation may also occur, whereby what are brutal and disgusting acts that fill the vast majority of us with a sense of shock and horror, are routine occurrences in the daily lives and minds of potential serial killers, and ones which bring them great pleasure and satisfaction.

As noted earlier, cruelty to animals and small children is commonly found in the serial killer's childhood. It is difficult to imagine the physical act of removing an animal's intestines and using them for the purposes of masturbation. It is repulsive. However, desensitisation means that as these individuals commit such acts more frequently, they grow used to them and feel less and less emotion each time, in much the same way as an abattoir worker eventually comes to feel nothing when an animal is killed. This process also occurs with cruelty to people. Repeated bullying and abusive behaviour allow these individuals to experience nothing except a feeling of power and control whenever another person suffers at their hands.

As the child becomes older, reaching the age of around 10 to 13 years old, they continue with this pattern of behaviour, all the while discovering that hurting other people is an extremely effective way of feeling good about themselves.

There is a downside to this behaviour for the potential serial killer, however. The more times the child bullies, inflicts pain on another and generally gets into trouble, the more socially isolated they become. The child is shunned and becomes an outcast. This reinforces their belief that they are alone in the world and they partake in ever more solitary activities, seeing people as merely objects around them rather than living and breathing human beings with their own emotions and feelings. The developing serial killer views the people around him as being mere players in a unique theatrical play, and never fully grasps the true reality of the world around him.

With the onset of puberty, the sexual element enters the equation. Witnessing their peers interacting with one another triggers their own sexual desires and urges. However, because they have been isolated for so long or because they are unsure of what true love and sharing really is, they become very frustrated.

The desire for sexual interaction is not eliminated, however, and it is at this stage that they begin to fantasise about owning another person sexually – controlling and dominating that other person in order to feel in a position of power themselves. They fantasise continually, engaging in autoerotic activity, with compulsive masturbation being common in 81 per cent of all offenders. Fetishes may develop. The use of pornography leads to new ideas being incorporated in the fantasy – although this does not cause the fantasy to become deviant in the first place. By mid to late adolescence, a seed has been planted for a deviant expression of sexuality, which may well be displayed and experienced later in life.

While obviously troubled, these individuals are relatively intelligent, as we have seen with Sam, at least insofar as to have the mental ability to conceal their real self from those around them for a prolonged period of time. Like him, they may also engage in 'normal' sexual relations later in life, but it is the combined feelings of power and control that they truly desire. As a result, they live their lives conning and manipulating people they are close to. They refine and further develop this deviant behaviour for later use.

Already Sam is looking for a suitable victim. As you read this, he is out there now, on a railway station platform, walking the street or standing at the bar, looking for someone, his excitement levels building as he sees the one he considers the perfect victim.

Sam says the reason he hasn't killed a person yet is because he is not completely convinced he will get away with it. While this could well be the case, it is more likely that Sam cannot focus his attention completely on the task at hand at present, but it is reasonably likely that one day he will try to kill.

Sam is a psychopath. He is a psychopath who has never been in trouble with the police. On the face of it, with his job, looks and charm, he lives a normal, effective life. He works hard, earns decent money, drives a nice car. Deep down, however, like so many of the sexual homicide offenders that have made headlines around the world, Sam is a chilling and manipulative, dishonest and self-serving coward, who doesn't have the capacity or desire to care about anyone but himself.

Only time will tell whether Sam becomes the world's latest serial killer. The path he is currently on is certainly leading him in this direction. Whether he can get help before it is too late remains to be seen. Whether that help will work is another matter. In our opinion, treatment is extremely unlikely to prove effective, as Sam does not want to change. Why would he, when he is perfectly content living the way he does? Sam has done nothing illegal at the present time. When he does, or attempts to, he will be caught. His behaviour is being monitored, and while we believe he has the potential to kill, whether he does or not is up to him. There's nothing we can do to stop this.

For the moment he remains on the hunt, waiting for his day. We hope that day never comes.

CHAPTER 2

Inside the Monster

Imagine it's raining outside as you lie on your bed reading a book, late on a wintry night. The wind is howling, it's cold out there and you're glad to be tucked up, warm and safe under the covers. You try and concentrate on your book and attempt to block out the whipping of the rain on your window that provides a steady backbeat to your attempt at pre-slumber relaxation.

The cacophony from the wind and rain prevents you from hearing the noise from the steady tap, tap, tapping at the foot of your bed. You put down your book and turn off the bedside light and try to sleep. Within minutes, with your brain no longer concentrating on the words of your favourite author, the tapping reaches your ears and you sit up and try to discover what it is.

Switching on the light, you look around the room, your hearing acute as you focus on uncovering the source of the noise. You glance up at the light in the ceiling and realise the problem in a split second. There's a steady flow of water leaking into your room from the attic and the water is coming through the hole in the ceiling where the cable for the light fitting exits. Instantly you realise what the real problem is – there is a hole in the roof, rainwater is spilling in, and coming into your room. Simple. Almost as instantly, you know how you are going to fix it, first so that it stops leaking now, and more importantly, so that it never happens again.

The analogy you've just read is a common life event. It shows how we as human beings approach problems by initially identifying the source of the problem and secondly seeking solutions to prevent their re-occurrence. It is our way of ensuring that life remains relatively normal, safe and enjoyable. It is a simple cognitive coping style common to a significant proportion of the population. Indeed, we live by certain rules.

The psychopath however, does not present us with a simple problem like the example above. By their very nature and actions, there is obviously something wrong with them – a significant psychological problem. But for this problem, as yet, there seems to be no real solution. We usually find it hard to identify psychopaths until it is too late, but we are making progress. However, sometimes we do come across someone who fits the clinical definition of a psychopath prior to them committing an offence – as in the case of Sam. Unfortunately, we are almost always unable to stop them from embarking upon their destructive behaviour. Why is this so? Basically because these people, like Sam, feel that their behaviour is justified, and have nothing but contempt for society and the people within it. More importantly, they are content with the way they live their lives. They have no inclination whatsoever to change. They are happy being the person they are. Merely thinking the way they do isn't illegal. Our hands are tied.

For many years a host of distinguished psychologists, psychiatrists, criminologists and law enforcement officials have attempted to uncover the inner workings of the minds of serial killers, rapists, stalkers and other psychopathic offenders. Their aim in doing this has been to make it easier to identify psychopaths and would-be psychopaths early, in the hope that their criminal careers can be nipped in the bud, and the safety of the general public improved. This study of the psychopathic mind has also had a huge impact on how major investigations are conducted.

Bookshelves are crammed with bestsellers from the likes of Paul Britton, Robert Keppel, John Douglas, Robert Ressler and Roy Hazelwood on the subjects of serial killers, rapists and stalkers, and in particular, on criminal profiling. Indeed the men mentioned above should be given due credit for making psychological and criminal profiling what it is today – a valuable, and often necessary, weapon used by police in capturing psychopathic offenders.

Aside from the normal investigative procedures employed by the police in hunting an unknown offender, there are times when an extra weapon in the fight against the psychopath is needed. There comes a time when, in order to understand the offender and thereby bring him to justice, we have to think like him. We have to get under his skin, into his mind. We achieve this by using offender profiling.

Offender profiling helps law enforcement officials gain specific information about the suspect that will aid in his eventual identification and arrest. It helps us discover who committed the crime through answering four vital questions – what happened, how, to whom, and why. It has been in use since the late 1950s and is utilised by law enforcement agencies around the world, as an integral part of the investigative process on select cases.

We'll look at offender profiling in greater depth in a later chapter. For the time being, to illustrate the type of information we need to ensure this vital investigative technique works to maximum effect, we'll concentrate on the characteristics of the two types of serial killer we know exist – the organised and disorganised offender. We'll then use a selected set of case studies to illustrate how profiling aids in psychologically pinpointing an offender.

An organised serial killer is a psychopathic offender who extensively plans and methodically executes his crimes. This is the offender who is the 'nice guy next door' who no one usually suspects of committing these sorts of crimes until they are caught. Of all the offenders described in this book, the organised serial killer fits the bill as a true psychopath – in every sense of the word – the best.

Usually of above average intelligence, and sometimes of genius level intelligence, the organised offender is extremely good at executing his crime. He plans his murderous endeavours meticulously, constantly going over the attack in his mind, fine-tuning the smallest of details so as to ensure that it meets with all of his expectations. Sam matches this clinical description of an organised offender in almost every way – the only exception being that he has yet to commit an offence.

Like Sam, the organised offender constantly fantasises about his crime. Compulsive masturbation would be a common factor in his life and his erotic fantasies would centre upon the sexual element of the murder. This would be the only way he could feel in control of his life. This is what he lives for, everything else is merely existing.

A special emotional significance is attached to the methodical planning and execution of the crime. It is the sole focus of the organised offender's life and the most pleasurable experience of their entire existence.

In some cases this offender type will stalk his victim extensively. He will know everything there is to know about her daily life. In other cases, he will stalk an area, searching for the perfect victim, the one that can fulfil his fantasy. Whatever stalking behaviour the offender partakes in, inevitably he will have carefully reconnoitred a site suitable for carrying out the crime, and will have mentally rehearsed the act multiple times.

When the time comes to finally fulfil his fantasy, the organised offender is as cunning and deceptive as he is thorough. He will approach his intended victim with confidence, using a ruse or a con to lure them into a trap. He will carry with him a selection of weapons, as well as a torture kit, and he will leave very little to chance. He will get his victim under his total control as soon as he possibly can. Then he will toy with them. Rape them. Beat them. And finally kill them. He'll then move the dead body to a separate dump-site well away from the scene of the murder. However, in some cases he will leave his lifeless victim where she is and position her in such a way as to send a message to society. For example, many victims are left in a state of undress in a range of sexually humiliating poses, the offender's intention being to imply that all women are worthless pieces of meat – every one of them a whore.

These men are human predators. Walking with them is like walking with the devil. This is how it feels.

You have grown up in an environment that is full of hurt and abuse. One where your parents have constantly neglected you, and have never made you feel special. You have never been loved and throughout your life you have learnt that if you want something, you simply go out and take it.

You have often heard other people talk about being frightened, but you have never experienced fear and this has given you an overwhelming sense of superiority. As far as you are concerned, there is nobody tougher, wiser, or maturer than yourself. The rest of the population are useless halfwits who have no idea how good you are.

You are easily bored. You like to break the rules. You cheat on your wife, you lie and steal because it feels good. You are the only person who sees the world for what it really is – a place where rules are made to be broken. And you are so good at it that you have never been caught. You just get better and better.

Because you get bored, you are constantly on the lookout for some excitement in your life. That's how it all happened, this killing spree. You were bored, you went out one evening and you saw her. You thought about her at night as you lay in bed. She excited you. You imagined what it would be like to take her, hurt her. It turned you on. You understand now that there is nothing more exciting than hunting and destroying other people. You are the only person that matters. You don't need to be told what to do, or how to act. This is your life and you will live it your way.

There are people you work with and live next to who look down on you. What a bunch of idiots they are, you constantly think to yourself. If only they knew what you did to their wives and girlfriends when it was dark and you were on the hunt. If only they knew the power you have, the hurt and pain you can cause. Then they would respect you. Then they would sit up and take notice. You get off on seeing the fear in their eyes whenever they read the newspapers and learn about another of your lovers. It inspires you to do more. Their reactions are to blame for what you do. You are faultless.

You live in a fantasy world, where you control everything. You have been doing as much since you were very young, around five or six. No one can hurt you in your world, no one can tell you what to do.

You have moulded yourself over the years into the person you are now. Your sexual fantasies were sated for a while with voyeurism and the odd rape. But you always knew that there was more. That night, on the disused railway line with the woman from the train you saw every day – that was the beginning of the bliss. You didn't mean to kill her. She fought you too hard. You were only trying to keep her still, control her, while you gave her what she wanted. It was an accident that you strangled her. It wasn't your fault that you couldn't help but have an intense orgasm as you saw her eyes roll back in her head and heard her last breath catch in her throat.

It was a rush you had never felt before. So satisfying. So real. So perfect. Since then you've been analysing what went wrong and how you can get more out of the next one. The pressures of life around you, the nagging wife, the demanding mistress, the boss – they're all getting to you. It's time to let off steam. It's time for another fix. Time to get another victim.

You know where you're going to go to find another girl. You know what she will look like, blonde like the first one, tall and slim. You've got some tools with you in a bag. Tools that will keep her quiet, give you more control. Ropes, knives, tape and hammer. All of them picked for the purpose of keeping her down, making her yours. You love the knife. You love the terror it brings. You're getting more excited thinking about it, thinking about number one, imagining an even better number two.

Your hunting ground is familiar territory to you. An easy 20-minute drive from work, you know the side streets, the bars, the cafes. You know where you'll dump the body, you picked the site two weeks ago when you went for a drive around the area.

A quick beer and you're ready. You need to be calm early on – you don't want to scare her too soon with the intensity of your eyes. That can come later. The bar is busy when you get there. But you see her. Same seat as last week, alone, looking for love and affection as she sips a drink and smokes a cigarette. She's even wearing the same shoes. You remember them from the week before. Your intelligence makes you smile.

You walk to where she's sitting at the bar and wait to be served. You drop your wallet on the floor next to her and accidentally nudge her leg as you go to pick it up. You apologise, smile that warm smile you practise each morning in the mirror, and then you start speaking to her. You're all good manners and polite conversation. It takes you less than 30 minutes to have her walk out of the bar with you towards your car and the tools. She thinks you're going to the club down the road. She thinks she's safe with you. She's wrong.

You pull out the knife as soon as you're next to the car and opening the door for her to get in. You catch that exciting look of terror in her eyes, the sheer helplessness. It's all so easy for you. You're right. People are stupid.

She's frozen in terror. You're all business. Quickly you tie her up and gag her mouth with the tape. She resists you eventually, but by then she has no hope. No one will miss her for the next few moments. She will be yours.

You tell her that she'll live if she stops struggling. Of course she stops. She doesn't want to imagine the worst – she wants to live. Compliant now, you drive her bound and gagged to the area of bush you prepared a month ago for this very moment. Nobody goes there. Nobody will hear her screams. No one will come to rescue her.

The excitement builds in you the more you hurt her. The

pain she expresses arouses you to bursting point. Nothing is this good. You feel like the most powerful being in the world. Nothing can stop you now. You are God. She needs you to live. You hold her life in your bloodied hands.

Her fear smells. It permeates everything around you. The time has come to fulfil the fantasy. You watch your hands clasp her neck. You watch her wince with pain, feel her shudder, hear that last agonising breath. Like the first one, her eyes stare at you, then roll back in her head. It's all too much for you, this moment. You ejaculate. You can't help it. The release is nerve tingling. The highest of highs.

You get rid of her body soon after, leaving her next to a rubbish bin, naked and with her legs spread for all of the world to see what a completely useless piece of rubbish she was, just like the rest of the female race.

You get to thinking of the next time. Maybe you should spend more time, get more from them. Maybe you shouldn't kill them so quickly. You decide to work on this while you're reliving the moments with number two in your head. In a couple of weeks you'll be ready again. There's no need to rush.

You keep her necklace, because it helps you to remember your moment together. You play with yourself looking at the necklace, recalling while you masturbate the power you had over her, the pain you made her feel. Will this ever stop? No. This is a drug for you now. You need it to survive.

The police have nothing on you, according to the local newspapers and TV bulletins. You keep the media clippings. They are your legacy to the world. You will be remembered as someone who held the power of life and death. You will be remembered as a god. You must do more, and you do. You are a serial killer now. You are a human hunter. You will not stop until you are caught or die.

You have just taken a journey into the mind of an organised serial killer. It is a mind infinitely complex, a world away from anything the overwhelming majority of us ever come into contact with. It is a mind still not yet fully understood by science or society. The fleeting glimpse we have just given you serves a number of purposes. For a start it enables you to understand the thought processes that consume such individuals. It does not provide excuses for their behaviour, but rather affords an insight into their typical personalities, backgrounds and motivations. But more importantly, what you have just read illustrates graphically how incredibly easy it is to become a victim of such an individual. It could happen when you least expect it. And when it does, you wouldn't realise until it was too late.

In terms of sophistication, the disorganised serial killer is on a different level to his organised cousin. This second type of offender is exactly what his name suggests – disorganised. He doesn't plan the attack in minute detail. He doesn't stalk his victim for weeks on end. He doesn't clean up after himself once he's finished.

There are a number of reasons as to what makes this type of offender so disorganised. The lack of sophistication evidenced can be the result of the person's lack of maturity in committing criminal acts, the influence of excessive amounts of drugs or alcohol, the offender's low level of intelligence, and occasionally, the presence of some form of mental disorder, such as schizophrenia.

A common thread that binds disorganised offenders together is the fact that in almost all cases they are uncomfortable dealing with their victim as a person. We know this by closely looking at the crime scene immediately following an attack. Whereas the organised offender will use a degree of cunning to entice his victim to be alone with him, the disorganised offender prefers to neutralise his victim quickly with a blitz-style attack. Their acute lack of oral and interpersonal skills makes this the only way they can efficiently capture their prey.

Again, in direct contrast to the organised offender, there is usually only one crime scene – the kill and body dump-sites being the same place. The victim may also be depersonalised in some manner. This depersonalisation allows the offender to maintain the belief that his victim is an object, not a human being like him. Typically the victim will be found with her face covered or badly beaten. In some cases she may be rolled onto her stomach, thus preventing her eyes from 'seeing' the offender.

Sexual acts will usually be performed on the victim while she is unconscious or dead. These sex acts will not necessarily involve intercourse. Rather they will consist of some form of necrophilia using an object to penetrate the victim other than the penis. The offender is incapable of dealing with a living, breathing human being and can only fulfil his bizarre needs with an immobile victim who is completely incapable of offering any resistance.

The offender's lack of sophistication is also displayed in the amount of forensic evidence left at the crime scene, and the fact that almost without fail he will not arrive at the scene with a weapon. He has not planned the crime well and will often find and use a suitable weapon at the crime scene, be it a knife, rock or the branch of a tree.

He may not be as sophisticated as the organised serial killer, but the disorganised offender is equally violent and a very real threat. Their killing regimes provide them with a purpose in life. Each victim satisfies the murderer's lust for power and control. Through the vicious murder of an innocent, they find a reason to live. We are all potential victims of this type of offender, and being aware that they are out there may help us to protect ourselves against them.

Case Study One

The year is 1942 and the world is at war. Throughout Europe families are being forced out of their homes and are fleeing the bullets and bombs, looking for safe havens. Across the Atlantic in the United States, thousands of young men are being conscripted into the army and trained for battle, before being shipped out to base camps around the world.

On the other side of the world in Australia, Melbourne is fast filling up with the hordes of refugees, and gum chewing, cigarette smoking American GIs. Myriad accents and foreign faces fill the streets and for a short time, the tragedy, death and destruction of war seem a long way away.

But all this is about to change in wartime Melbourne. Death and destruction in the shape of a psychopathic killer are set to hit the streets. For 16 days, a sense of terror strikes the bustling city. Female residents live in fear of the depraved killer that is stalking their streets, and the local police are dumbfounded at the severity of the murders of three respected local women.

The first body is discovered dumped in a doorway in East Melbourne's Victoria Avenue on May 3. The victim is a 40-year-old domestic servant named Ivy McLeod. She is found with a fractured skull, multiple bruises to her head and body, and with her clothes ripped and torn to such an extent that on first inspection it looks like the unfortunate woman has been attacked by a wild animal. Despite the extent of her injuries and her naked appearance, McLeod has not been sexually molested or assaulted and there is small change in her purse totalling just over £1 in value.

Beginning our profile it is apparent that McLeod was in the wrong place at the wrong time. It is almost certain that she was followed for a short time, confronted and killed shortly afterward.

When approached by her killer, McLeod would have felt at ease. He would have come across as being trustworthy and would be a good talker. Once his victim was comfortable with his presence, our offender would have lured her into a place he felt safe in and committed his destructive act.

The absence of sexual assault is not necessarily unusual, given that the act is more about power, control and domination than about sexual gratification. We can see in this case the manifestation of an incredible rage directed against the female victim. The rage inside the killer explodes resulting in the savage beating and tragic appearance of the victim. The destructive motive for the attack is also made more clear by the fact that McLeod's purse was not stolen. It is obvious to us, even at this early stage, that we are not seeing a robbery gone wrong. We are dealing with a savage and brutal killer who will more than likely kill again.

Five days later another body is found dumped in similar circumstances. Stenographer Pauline Thompson, a 31-year-old mother of two, is discovered at 4 am on the steps of Morningside House in the city's Spring Street. Like McLeod she has been strangled with immense ferocity. Her clothing has been torn and ripped from her body leaving deep lacerations, and her face has been badly battered. Again, like McLeod, a post-mortem reveals that Thompson has not been sexually assaulted.

Thompson's husband is a police constable and has recently been posted to Bendigo. When he is later interviewed by homicide detectives he reveals that his wife had told him she was going to a dance at the Music Lovers' Club with a number of friends and a young GI called Justin Jones the evening of her death. She had planned to meet Jones at the American Hospitality Club before the dance. When he failed to arrive at the appointed hour of 7 pm, she gave up on him. According to witnesses she was last seen with another GI in the nearby Astoria Hotel. Thompson and the GI were seen leaving together at midnight.

The Melbourne media go into a frenzy following the discovery of the second murder victim, nicknaming the killer the Brownout Strangler on account of the fact that the murders had all been carried out during the so-called 'brownout' period – the partial blackout that hits the city at night as per wartime security.

At this point the killer will be following the media coverage of the murders very closely. There will be two reasons for this.

Firstly, he will be eager to know what evidence, if any, the police have with regard to apprehending the offender. More importantly, however, the attention given to the murders in the newpapers would reinforce the killer's feelings of power and importance. He would now know that an entire city is gripped with fear and panic solely because of him. Women are terrified. Knowing this is extremely rewarding for him. He feels the need to destroy women, perhaps as a result of something that has happened earlier in his life. What cannot be dismissed is the sorry state in which he leaves his victims. They are humiliated in death, left exposed for all to see. He is sending a powerful message to the residents of Melbourne – he hates women, and he wants to destroy them all.

The media erupts into an even bigger frenzy on the morning of May 19 with the discovery of the Brownout Strangler's third victim, 40-year-old Melbourne University librarian Gladys Hosking. Hosking has been strangled, beaten and stripped of her clothes. Like the two victims before her she has not been sexually assaulted. The evening before, Hosking and her friend Dorothy Pettigrew had left the university and headed home. After the two had gone their separate ways, Hosking huddled under her umbrella and was approached by a young and good looking GI who asked her if he could share her shelter from the lashing rain. She said yes and was last seen by witnesses walking with the GI towards Royal Park. Her body was found, covered in thick mud, within easy walking distance of the American Army base at Camp Pell.

At this point we would conclude in a profile that the killer would be between the ages of 20 to 30, probably closer to his mid- to late-20s given the frequency of the murders and the accomplished nature with which they are done. However, the destruction of the bodies post-mortem, and certain behavioural patterns, are still not fully developed for this offender, making him possibly even younger. He would most likely be living somewhere near to where each of the bodies were found, especially given the movement restrictions in the wartime environment and the ease with which he simply dumps the bodies and disappears. He would be of a similar socioeconomic status to the victims, given that he is able to talk to them on a similar level, and make them feel at ease. It is likely he would have used alcohol prior to committing the crimes, given the uninhibited nature of the attack patterns. He would probably have a full-time job during the day, which is why all of the victims are killed late at night. The police would be wise to investigate men who fit this particular profile who work near to the crime scenes – certainly American GIs on the nearby base.

With the witness statements regarding the GI, the police now have a lead. They get their man when they visit Camp Pell on May 20 and hear Private Noel Seymour, an Australian soldier on sentry duty the night of the third murder, relate an incident that had occurred in the early hours of May 19. According to Private Seymour, a staggering and mud covered GI had arrived at the gates of the camp just after midnight. The American told the sentry that he was drunk and had fallen in some mud while walking through Royal Park.

Immediately after hearing Seymour's story, all 15,000 of the camp's soldiers are lined up on the parade ground and with police in tow, Seymour walks the lines. After a short while he stops in front of a 24-year-old Texan named Edward Joseph Leonski, and identifies him as the mud covered GI he had seen at the sentry gate. Within hours, Leonski admits that he is the savage killer that has terrorised the city for over a fortnight.

Leonski was tall and powerfully built. He was regarded as an odd individual and someone to be avoided when drunk. His background was less than idyllic. He came from a broken home. His father was an alcoholic who eventually drank himself to death. His mother was a professional female weightlifter who went from one bad romance to the next.

Despite his turbulent upbringing, Leonski was an honours student and had a healthy interest in the arts and music. His particular love was singing. However, Leonski was prone to deep and dark bouts of depression, which he would try to relieve with drinking binges. More often than not, these drinking sessions would turn violent. All his victims were killed following just such drinking sessions.

In his billet at Camp Pell, Leonski kept clippings of the newspaper reports about the murders and even told his closest friend that he was the Brownout Strangler. 'Everybody is wondering about these murders,' he told the friend. 'I'm not wondering, I know.'

Having been tried and convicted of the murders, Leonski was sentenced to death by hanging. General Douglas MacArthur confirmed the sentence on November 4, and the Brownout Strangler was hung at Pentridge Prison five days later.

Case Study Two

It's a Sydney suburb that has it all and comes complete with a genuine feeling of security. Situated just minutes from the excitement of the CBD, nearby pristine beaches and the glittering waters of the harbour, Mosman is one of the gems of the city's affluent North Shore.

Its sense of safety and plentiful amenities have made it a popular place for retirees, and the area's relatively low level of crime enhances its appeal. It is an exclusive enclave and is home to some of the city's most stunning and expensive homes. Locals will tell you that it is a tranquil place where bad things tend not to happen. But they are wrong.

Mosman has its dark side and for a year-long period between March 1989 and March 1990, the suburb provided the killing ground to one of Australia's worst and possibly most callous psychopathic serial murderers. This killer was also brazen, murdering all of his victims during the day and almost always attacking them outdoors as they walked Mosman's leafy streets.

Gwendoline Mitchelhill was the killer's first victim, losing her life on 1 March. A frail old woman, she was attacked metres from the ever-busy Military Road in the entry foyer of her Mosman retirement village. The killer struck as she turned the key in the lock, hitting her on the back of the head with a hammer. As she fell to the ground, the killer continued to lash out at her with the hammer, hitting Mitchelhill so hard that he broke several of her ribs. With his victim lying in a pool of blood on the floor, the killer then calmly bent down and stole her purse containing $100.

Just over two months later, the killer struck again. Lady Winifred Ashton, aged 84, was returning home from the Mosman RSL club where she had been playing bingo. She was followed to her home in nearby Raglan Street by the killer. She made it as far as the foyer of her unit before she was struck repeatedly on the back of the head with a hammer by her assailant. She was beaten unconscious, dumped in the rubbish-bin alcove and strangled with her pantyhose. Her shoes and walking stick were placed neatly by her feet and her purse was stolen. Despite the severity of the attack, and the fact that her underwear and tights had been removed, there was no sign of a sexual assault having taken place.

Why does this killer target older women? This is one of the most important questions we must ask when embarking on a profile for this case. The offender's motivation for such brutal attacks could be that he hates his mother or that he hates older women in general. One reason for this might be that he is dominated by an older woman in his life, someone who he feels has ruined him, mentally and physically.

The level of ill feeling is obviously high, with the offender committing what is a very personal and brutal attack with a hammer. To do this he must get close to his victim. The fact that one victim was strangled adds to the personal nature of the crime.

In general, attacks of this nature on elderly females are carried out by young male offenders. However, this is not the case in this instance. There is a level of hatred and confidence that implies that these crimes have been committed by an experienced attacker who feels comfortable brutalising older women. This displays experience, and it is likely that the offender has a history of assaulting older females.

Taken by themselves, the crime scenes offer us even more information about the killer. He appears to be familiar with the area, and despite the fact that the attacks are high-risk (carried out in daylight in full view of residences etc), he is not overly concerned with this. The lack of physical evidence tells us that the offender is not disorganised, or an amateur. This vital clue confirms our theory about the age of the offender. His familiarity with the crime scenes leads us to believe that he probably lives near to the areas where the crimes are committed. He may pass through the area every day for a variety of reasons and feel very comfortable committing his crimes there, as he knows Mosman like the back of his hand.

Ashton's death prompted the police to fear that they might be dealing with a serial killer. Their suspicions were made stronger when they checked local crime reports and discovered a number of previous attacks on old women in the area. In one, 84-year-old Margaret Todhunter was attacked as she walked along Hale Road. Todhunter's assailant punched her in the face and grabbed her handbag before running off. Police now suspected that Todhunter had gotten off lightly and that there was a strong chance that her attacker was the same man that had killed Mitchelhill and Ashton later in the year.

When called in to assist with such a case, a profiler would tell the investigating officers to check their databases for similar attacks on older females in the recent past. The reason for this is simple. An offender of this type doesn't simply wake up one morning and suddenly decide to go out and kill a pensioner. It is something that he has progressed to, over a period of time. This is the culmination of his psychopathic education.

The media latched on to the killings and immediately dubbed the man responsible the Granny Killer. As the news bulletins gave the case huge coverage and Mosman's locals struggled to come to terms with the fact that they were living under the shadow of a possible serial killer, the police realised that they were definitely dealing with one suspect on October 18.

At the time of her attack, Doris Cox was an 86-year-old suffering from Alzheimer's disease. She was slowly making her way along Spit Road when she was approached by a man, who began to walk with Cox towards her retirement village. As the pair entered the stairwell that led to Cox's unit, the man attacked her from behind, using his whole weight to pin her against the wall. He then beat her about the head and face until she collapsed. Having rifled through her handbag and purse and finding nothing that he wanted, the attacker made off and left her for dead.

Amazingly, Cox survived the attack, but could not give a firm description of the man that had beaten her within inches of her life. She did however tell police that she thought her attacker was a young male.

Margaret Pahud, aged 85, was not so lucky. On November 2 she was found dead by a passing schoolgirl in a laneway off busy Longueville Road in Lane Cove, some 5 km from Mosman. Pahud had been killed as a result of repeated blows to the head from a blunt instrument. Her skull was shattered by the force of the attack and she was dead before she hit the ground. Her purse had been stolen.

Just 24 hours later, the Granny Killer's fifth victim was discovered. Olive Cleveland, aged 81, was found dead in a secluded walkway in the grounds of the Wesley Gardens Retirement Village in Belrose, an upper North Shore enclave within easy reach of Mosman. She was found with massive head injuries and her pantyhose knotted tightly around her neck.

November 24 saw yet another body turn up in Mosman. Muriel Falconer was 92 at the time of her death and partially deaf and blind. She was attacked in her home with a hammer to the head and neck. Falconer was then strangled with her pantyhose as she lay dying on the floor. A bloodied footprint, belonging to the killer, sat next to the body of the Granny Killer's sixth victim.

At this point the killer would be full of confidence. In his mind, he would be invincible. He has got away with six murders and the police are far from knowing who he is. He would probably be in a relationship with a more submissive female, who would have no idea as to his identity, another fact that would please him greatly. He would be conning the world, and getting away with it.

The rage within him to commit more murders would be growing stronger every day. He will need to do more. The satisfaction he gains from the killings is not lasting very long and he is addicted to the thrill. While he may derive some shallow pleasure from his acts, deep down he is still insecure about himself and unable to completely fulfil the cravings that cause him to kill. Hence the repeated murders in such a short timeframe.

He will be stressed, not through fear of being captured, but because the rage inside him is slowly consuming him whole and nothing he does to stop it seems effective. It is unlikely that he will stop killing old women, as the murders allow him to fulfil his needs. To those around him, he would appear normal, albeit a little stressed. The people witnessing this stress would not attribute it to being caused by the murders. They would not suspect their husband, father, brother or son as being the Granny Killer.

The big break in the police case came on January 11. A heavy set, grey-haired man in his fifties walked into one of the wards at Greenwich Hospital where four old and very sick women lay in their beds. The man approached one of the women, lifted the sheets from off the bed, and began fondling her under the bedclothes.

The elderly patient managed to alert nursing staff via an emergency buzzer. One of the ward sisters answered the call and confronted the man who barged past her and ran out of the building. The sister chased after him and managed to take down the registration number of the man's car as he sped out of the car park.

Three weeks went by before the police investigating the Granny Killer were told of the incident. When they were, they finally had a name of a suspect – John Wayne Glover, a seemingly friendly fifty-something pie salesman from Mosman. Detectives immediately went to question Glover at his home, but were told that their chief suspect was in hospital, after having attempted suicide. Arriving at the hospital later that evening, nursing staff handed the police a suicide note written by Glover that included the words 'no more grannies …'.

Glover was questioned and placed under surveillance until more evidence could be compiled against him. On the morning of March 19, 1990, Glover visited the house of a female acquaintance, Joan Sinclair. Detectives followed him to the Mosman address and waited for their suspect to reappear.

'It was a very stressful moment,' Detective Sergeant Paul Jacob, one of the officers outside the house that day, told us. 'We believed he was meeting someone he knew and when he was greeted at the door with a kiss by Ms Sinclair, we had no reason to suspect that anything untoward was going to happen. Everything seemed okay. However, as the time passed we became increasingly concerned and that's when we moved in.'

With guns drawn, Jacob and his colleagues, Detective Sergeant Miles O'Toole and Detective Paul Mayger, entered the house. 'Knowing that he [Glover] was in there heightened the stress levels,' Jacob said. 'I'll never forget looking into the house for the first time and seeing a hammer lying on the floor covered with blood. I looked to my right and could see the poor woman. The bottom half of her body was exposed and she'd been violated. Her head was severely battered and had been covered with towels. They were soaked with blood.'

The three officers crept quietly through the living room and came to the bathroom.

'Glover was lying naked in the bath,' Jacob said. 'He had slashed one of his wrists, he felt cold and there was an empty bottle of Scotch on the floor. We checked his vital signs and found that he was alive.'

Later, Jacob interviewed Glover about his killing spree. 'He was very cold and calculated,' Jacob said. 'He talked in a matter of fact way and spoke of the murders and his actions as if what he'd done was as normal as selling a pie.'

Glover, the Granny Killer, was charged with the deaths of six women. His brush with the law was not his first. In fact, Glover had a hefty criminal record dating as far back as 1947. He was a convicted thief and had a history of assaulting females. According to his testimony at trial, Glover had an intense hatred of his mother-in-law. Glover also loathed his mother, who died of breast cancer in 1988. She had been living with Glover and his wife, daughters and mother-in-law at his Mosman home. However, at his instigation, she was moved to Gosford, 100 km north of Sydney, when her cancer grew life-threatening. In a bizarre twist – and what a leading psychiatrist described to the court as '[his mother] reaching out and striking him again from the grave' – Glover was also diagnosed as suffering from breast cancer, an extremely rare condition in men. He would later develop a prostate condition, which led to him becoming sexually impotent.

In November 1991, John Wayne Glover was sentenced to six life terms of imprisonment after jurors took just two-and-a-half hours to decide his fate. He is never to be released.

CHAPTER 3

Dennis Nilsen: A Lonely Man
with a Deadly Mission

O f all the convicted serial killers there are living in our
world today, one in particular, for me at least, stands
apart from the rest. His story could be the stuff of
fiction. It is sad, revolting, fascinating and frightening. If it was
a novel, make no bones about it, it'd be a bestseller.

This particular killer's words, poems, pencil drawings, private
thoughts made public, all add a mystical and tragic edge to this
particularly disturbing tale, and have allowed us to journey
inside the life and mind of a sadistic killer. The subject of this
chapter was a lonely man in need of love and affection. But do
not pity him. He was a lonely man who knew his limitations in
attracting and securing that love and affection. He was a lonely
man who made an evil choice. He killed for company. His name
is Dennis Nilsen.

If you ever wanted to know how it feels to kill, how it feels to
take a life, then the text (disturbing in some parts) you are about
to read, more than any other in this book, will show you. For the

words, the actions described, are Nilsen's own. He likes to talk does Dennis Andrew Nilsen. And ever since his arrest on February 9, 1983, this unremarkable man in every other aspect of his life, with a remarkable lust for blood, has been telling anybody who'll listen why and how he managed to kill 15 young men over a period of just four years – his words are chilling and enthralling and offer a real insight into the obscure mind of a serial killer

Dennis Nilsen was born on 23 November, 1945, of a Scottish mother and Norwegian father in a tiny room at 47 Academy Road in the town of Fraserburgh on the north-easterly tip of Aberdeenshire. His personality was moulded by the place of his birth and many of the psychological characteristics he would display later in life had their genesis in Fraserburgh. Back then it was a town of rugged sea-faring people, all of them shaped by the strong buffeting winds and frequently fierce waters of the North Sea, and each one of them possessing a bluntness of nature that Nilsen himself would show all too clearly some 37 years later following his arrest.

Like many other serial killers and psychopathic offenders before him, it was his formative years that helped shape Nilsen and his future. In fact, if we step back in time and look at the first decade of his life there are a number of key events which, when analysed carefully, help provide some answers as to why he did what he did.

Three years before his birth, Nilsen's mother – a headstrong girl named Betty Whyte – and father – a Norwegian Army officer named Olav Magnus Nilsen – had met by chance when Olav had rescued the attractive Betty from the aggressive and unwanted advances of another soldier as she made her way home from an evening out at a local café. Falling head over heels in love with her rescuer, Betty Whyte ignored her parent's protests and on 2 May, 1942 married Olav Nilsen.

It was a wartime marriage, and Olav had pressing military responsibilities and from the start, the young couple spent protracted periods of time away from one another. In truth, the marriage was a mistake, one based more on lust than love. As such, Betty and Olav never formed a family unit or built a home together. The world was in turmoil around them and this, coupled with their inability to share more than a few days leave together, meant that their three children, Olav Jnr, Dennis and Sylvia, were raised by Betty alone, with only the help of her parents in whose house the young Nilsen family resided. Betty and Olav eventually divorced in 1948 and Dennis Nilsen never saw his father. His life was dysfunctional even while he was in his mother's womb and this, coupled with the fact that he never really got along with his siblings, led him to feel like he was the misfit of the family.

Dennis Nilsen had what could be best be described as a troubled childhood. He never saw his father, he was a broody and often ill-mannered boy who was secretive in nature and always a loner. But he did have one friend and confidant. His grandfather, Andrew, a well-respected local fisherman, with whom he had a special bond. A man he worshiped.

'I remember being borne aloft on the tall, strong shoulders of my great hero and protector, my grandfather,' Nilsen would write over 30 years later following his conviction.

31 October, 1951 proved to be a life-changing day for the young and impressionable Dennis Nilsen. For that was the day,

that for him at least, the music of his life died. At the age of 62, Andrew Whyte passed away, leaving behind a void that was never filled for Nilsen. In the blink of an eye, Dennis Nilsen's guiding light and one true friend, his hero, had gone. The last time he saw his grandfather was when Betty Whyte showed her son his dead body as it lay in an open coffin in the Academy Road living room where Nilsen himself had been born. It was an image, and a loss, that rocked Nilsen's world and one that he never got over.

'My troubles started there. It blighted my personality permanently,' he recalled.

Nilsen is telling the truth. From that moment on he was impossible to control. His mother had little or no influence over him. With no father figure with which he could associate and learn from, Nilsen spent an increasing amount of time alone, with only his own mind for company. 'On occasion I was a difficult child to manage. I was a very lonely and turbulent child. I inhabited my own secret world full of ideal and imaginary friends.'

Bored with his life, and increasingly jealous of his mother's new husband, Adam Scott, and the place his step-father had in her affections, Dennis Nilsen looked for other ways in which to rid himself of the boredom of his everyday existence. At the age of 15 he found the one thing that he thought could give him the guidance and discipline he needed. The Army. In September 1961 he arrived in Aldershot with only a battered suitcase for company and signed on for a nine-year stint of duty with the Army Catering Corps.

Nilsen was an exemplary soldier and quickly made a name

for himself as a dependable sort, who worked hard and fitted in well with the highly disciplined way of military life, which is not surprising as it was this aspect of the Army that had perhaps appealed to him the most. He was good at his job. Perhaps he was too good, for it was here that his skills with a knife and his deadly knowledge of skinning and cutting up joints of meat was honed.

It was also in the Army Catering Corps that Dennis Nilsen first discovered his latent homosexuality. More interestingly, as he would reveal from his prison cell it was around this time that during private moments alone, he first experimented sexually with himself and became fascinated by the pallor of death. Even more interestingly, it was during this time, at the age of 22, that he began acting out a fantasy that would recur throughout his life and be one of the most shocking aspects of his crimes when it was discussed during his trial some 20 years later.

'The novelty of one's own body soon wore off,' he admitted. 'I needed something positive to relate to. My imagination hit on the idea of using a mirror. By placing a large, long mirror on its side beside the bed, I would view my own reclining reflection. At first I was always careful not to show my head, because the situation needed that I believe it was someone else. I would give the reflection some animation, but that play could not be drawn out too long. The fantasy could dwell much longer on a mirror image which was asleep.'

Years later Nilsen, living and working in London and becoming increasingly depressed, lonely and reliant on his fantasy world, would add a bizarre twist to his mirror routine.

'In the lonely years I became more and more into myself and

expressed my fantasies of physical love on my own body. My most fulfilling sexual feasts were savoured with the image of myself in the mirror. It evolved from being an unconscious body to a dead body.'

This fantasy completely overwhelmed him and for Nilsen the image of the dead body in the mirror became his sole focus, his reason for living. But what he was seeing still wasn't enough. He therefore took the fantasy a step further. It was easy to lie still and watch with increasing sexual arousal his hands moving slowly over the 'dead' body, but there was something missing. He remembered how his grandfather had looked in his coffin all those years ago. The ashen colour of his skin. Nilsen, fuelling the fantasy still some more, replicated this colour of death – by covering himself in talc to 'erase the living colour', applying charcoal under his eyes to 'accentuate a hollow, dark look' and putting pale blue on his lips to add to the overall dead affect.

As his private life took a turn for the worse, so too did his professional life. By the late-70s, Nilsen had left the Army, joined and left the Metropolitan Police (he was Police Constable Q287 based at Willesden Green Police Station, London, between 1972 and 1973) and had begun working for the Department of Employment. He was an active trades unionist, with an irritable temper, but nevertheless was someone who often thought of others before himself and was one of the most popular employee representatives during dispute cases in the area. However perhaps because of his union activities, as well as his forthright manner and personality, he was continually passed over for promotion and this irritated and angered him. It also did nothing for his self-esteem, which by 1978, following a string of failed relationships and emotional pain, was at its lowest ebb.

With the fantasies of his mind running riot, it was therefore not surprising that in a matter of time the dam that was holding all his hate and discontent back would break and all hell would be let loose – he would outgrow the fantasy and inner rage, and cross the line between right and wrong. It was time to get even with the society that was shunning him. Time to move on.

In need of company, desperate for someone to share his bizarre fantasies with, Dennis Nilsen went on the hunt. He was a dangerous stranger, living alone, and totally demoralised. It could only lead to one thing. There was no stopping him. He began his new life as a murderer on 30 December, 1978.

His first victim was a young Irishman he met in the Cricklewood Arms in North London. They drank together that evening, both of them knocking back pint after pint of Guinness, until drunk, Nilsen invited the man to his ground floor flat at 195 Melrose Avenue, Willseden Green. On arrival, they both undressed and stumbled into bed, where they slept together, but, according to Nilsen, no sexual activity took place. A couple of hours later, Dennis Nilsen awoke, aroused by the sight and touch of the naked body beside him, his heart pounding in his chest, sweat beading his forehead, a fear of loneliness coursing through his veins.

Nilsen tried to calm himself down. He was afraid that if he woke the sleeping man next to him, he would leave. Spotting the pile of discarded clothes on the floor beside the bed, Nilsen noticed his tie and thought of a way in which he could force the man to stay – by killing him.

'I reached out and got the tie. I raised myself and slipped it on under his neck. I quickly straddled him and pulled tight for all I was worth. His body came alive immediately. We struggled off the bed onto the floor. We moved along the carpeted floor. We moved from the bed. His head was now up against the wall. After about half a minute I felt him slowly going limp. His arms flopped to the carpet.'

Trembling with nerves, Nilsen panicked and wondered what to do next. The man was not yet dead, although he was having difficulty breathing. Knowing that he must do something, Nilsen ran into his kitchen, filled a bucket full of water and returned to the man.

'I got hold of him under his armpits and pulled him up and draped him head down over the seat of a dining chair. I placed the bucket near by and grabbing him by the hair raised his head, which I pushed into the bucket of water. I held his head in there and he did not struggle.'

Nilsen went through what would go on to become a ritual with all of his unfortunate victims. First he bathed the man. Then he towelled him dry. Then he carried him into his bedroom and laid him down on the bed.

'I dressed him in Y-fronts, vest and socks and put back the bedclothes. I had a bath' myself and got into bed with him. I held him close to me with my arms around him and I began to remove his pants and explore his body under the blankets. I had an erection all this time. When I tried to enter him my erection automatically subsided.'

The man's body was placed under the floorboards of the flat. It stayed there for over seven months, until Nilsen removed it and burnt on a bonfire in his back garden on 11 August, 1979.

'It was the beginning of the end of my life,' he said later. 'I had started down the avenue of death and possession of a new kind of flat mate.'

Astonished that he was able to get away with something like this, Nilsen believed at the time that he would never commit such an act again. But Nilsen's continuum of violence together with the fact that he saw his actions as his way of getting back at society would never allow this to happen. Over the next two years, Dennis Nilsen would kill another 12 young men at Melrose Avenue, each of them murdered in the same ritualistic manner. And as we have seen countless times before, and have read in this book, the level of violence exhibited by Nilsen during these lethal rituals increased with each and every one.

It could be argued that what Nilsen did to many of his victims – he dismembered their bodies and boiled their heads in pots – was done with a purely logistical perspective. He'd killed so many men and buried them all beneath his floorboards that depositing the cadavers of his latest victims was becoming increasingly difficult. This could well be the case, but as we have learnt, one of the key psychological drivers in any criminal of Nilsen's type is the desire to gain complete dominance, power and control over their helpless and incapacitated victim. And there is no better way to do this than by totally dehumanising that victim and treating them like a piece of rotten meat. Remember, Dennis Nilsen had learnt all about butchering during his years in the Catering Corps. He knew how best to cut up a body and remove its organs. It also thrilled him to have this much power over his victims. His was not a logistical choice. It was a purely pathological one. Psychopathic, in fact, in its intensity. For Dennis Nilsen, dismembering his victims was as easy as going for a walk in the park with his dog, Bleep (which incidentally is what he often did immediately afterwards).

I'd pull up the body from the floorboards and along into the kitchen onto some plastic sheeting. I got ready a small bowl of water, a kitchen knife, some paper tissues and plastic bags. With the knife I cut the head from the body. There was very little blood. I put the head in the kitchen sink, washed it and put it in a carrier bag. I then cut off the hands, then the feet. I washed them in the sink and dried them. I made a cut from the body's navel to the breast bone. I removed all the intestines, stomach, kidneys and liver. I would break through the diaphragm and remove the lungs and heart. I put all these organs into a plastic carrier bag. I then separated the top half of the body from the bottom half. I removed the arms and then the legs below the knee. I put the chest and ribcage in a large bag and the thighs, buttocks, and private parts in another. I stored the packages back under the floorboards. After I replaced the packages under the floor I had a bath. Afterwards I would listen to music on the headphones or take Bleep out for a walk.

Nilsen moved from Melrose Avenue shortly after he had burnt whatever remained of the 12 dead bodies entombed beneath his living room floor. Incredibly his move came about following a burglary at his house during which the majority of his possessions had been vandalised. His landlords weren't all that sorry to see him go – he had been a notoriously difficult tenant and was behind on his rent – and after packing what few intact possessions he now owned into plastic bags, Dennis Nilsen moved to nearby 23 Cranley Gardens on 5 October, 1981.

'Driving away from Melrose Avenue was a great relief,' Nilsen recalled in a diary he wrote following his arrest.

He rented an attic flat, which prophetically had no floorboards to bury bodies under and no garden in which to set them alight. Nilsen vainly hoped that the move would put an end to his murderous lifestyle, but it was a forlorn dream – three men were strangled at 23 Cranley Gardens in March and September of 1982 and January of 1983. The disposal and subsequent discovery of their bodies would be Nilsen's downfall.

A blocked drain in the Cranley Gardens apartment block was what set in motion a chain of events that would horrify the British public. On February 8, 1983, Michael Cattran a 30-year-old Dyno-Rod technician, arrived at 23 Cranley Gardens to fix the blocked drain. With the help of another resident, Jim Allcock, Cattran lowered himself through a manhole cover that led to the sewers and outlet pipes below the small block. The pair noticed a peculiar and revolting smell. Shining his torch into the hole, Cattran glimpsed a porridge-like syrup on the floor of the sewer, some eight or nine inches thick, composed of about 30 or 40 pieces of what looked like greyish-white flesh. Cattran, a newcomer to the job, knew that this was something he should report to his supervisor, so, hauling himself back up, he replaced the manhole cover and left to contact his boss.

Dennis Nilsen had watched this commotion carefully.

Knowing that the blocked drain had been caused by his flushing pieces of bone and flesh down the toilet of his flat, under cover of darkness he scrambled down into the sewer, removed the human remains and dumped them over the garden hedge. When Cattran and his supervisor returned the next morning, they were shocked and surprised to see that the mess had vanished. Unabashed, Cattran climbed back into the hole and felt around an outlet pipe from which he retrieved small pieces of bone and bits of flesh.

Unware to Nilsen, his neighbour, Fiona Bridges, had heard him walking down the stairs of 23 Cranley Gardens the night before and had listened to him fumbling with the manhole cover. Feeling increasingly uncomfortable with what was transpiring, Allcock and Bridges, together with Cattran, telephoned the police.

While this was going on, Dennis Nilsen was dong his best to get through what he suspected would be his last day at his desk at Kentish Town Jobcentre. It was February 9, 1983. A day that Nilsen described as 'the day help arrived'. He seemed distant that day, according to his colleagues, as if something else was on his mind. Not the usual Dennis, they said. How right they were. Before leaving his desk that night, Nilsen, by now well-aware of his fate and what lay on store for him that evening, turned to his assistant, Don Stow, and said, 'If I am not in tomorrow, I will either be ill, dead, or in jail.' They both laughed.

Waiting just inside the front door of the Cranley Gardens hallway was Detective Chief Inspector Peter Jay, who knew all about the flesh that had been found. He'd arrived at Cranley Gardens at 11am, had seen the flesh and bones and had taken them to Charing Cross Hospital, where David Bowen, Professor of Forensic Medicine at the University of London, had examined them and determined that the tissue was indeed human and had come from a man's neck. The bones were more than likely from a man's hand, according to Professor Bowen. Together with Detective Inspector Stephen McCusker and Detective Constable Jeffrey Butler, DCI Jay returned to Cranley Gardens and waited for Dennis Nilsen to return from work. He arrived, a tin of dog food in his hand, at 5.40pm.

'We've come about the drains,' DCI Jay told Nilsen, to which the murderer expressed surprise. All four men then walked up the stairs to Nilsen's flat. Once inside, DCI Jay informed Nilsen that he was interested in the drains because they'd been found to contain human remains. Nilsen expressed his horror at this shocking news.

'Don't mess about,' DCI Jay told him, not convinced by Nilsen's theatrics. 'Where's the rest of the body?'

The reply was calm and shocking in its simplicity.

'In two plastic bags in the wardrobe next door,' Nilsen said. 'I'll show you.'

One of the most astonishing facts about the Dennis Nilsen case is that fact that during those deadly four years, he somehow managed to maintain a normal everyday existence beyond the confines of his Melrose Avenue and later Cranley Gardens domains. But perhaps this is not so shocking as we know that such offenders have the ability to easily separate their criminal lives from their normal lives. In the same way that a rapist may well have a loving and unsuspecting wife at home during his crime spree, it is not therefore not surprising that a man as unassuming, intense and solitary as Dennis Nilsen could go undetected and unsuspected for so long.

Nilsen's lawyers argued long and hard that their client was not in full control of his mental faculties at the time of the murders – in a nutshell, he was insane and had no idea what he was doing. But listen to his words and you see a mind that is clear and lucid. Nilsen knew exactly what he was doing. He did all he could to hide the bodies of those he killed. And despite his protests that he battled constantly with himself over his actions, it took the police finding him for him to stop. Surely, if his inner turmoil was so strong, then it would have been easier for him to simply walk into a police station on December 31, 1978 and turn himself in? But he didn't. He didn't because he enjoyed what he did. He was a lonely and pathetic man who 'enjoyed' the company of 15 desperately sad and unfortunate young men. If you have any doubt, read these final words and judge for yourself the state of mind of Dennis Andrew Nilsen, one of Britain's most notorious killers:

'Words like "sorry" hold little comfort for the bereaved. I mistrust my own inner sincerity to bear even to utter them.'

On Friday, 4 November 1983, at just after 4.30 in the afternoon, Dennis Nilsen was found guilty of murder six times and of attempted murder twice. He was sentenced to life imprisonment with a recommendation that he serve a minimum of 25 years. To this day, he has remained aloof from the horrors of his crimes.

CHAPTER 4

Sex as a Weapon
– Rapists

Rape is the crime women fear the most and live in dread of. This is one of the most violent acts, and it repulses and terrifies like no other. Legally, rape is defined as the penetration of the mouth, vagina or anus by any part of an attacker's body or by an object used by an attacker without the consent of the victim.

Like all definitions of violent sexually motivated crime, the one just outlined for rape is cold and precise. The physical act is just as cold, but is crueller, more evil and more life changing than mere words can define.

Even the very thought of being the victim of a rapist changes the way women live their lives. They are constricted and restricted in what they do, who they talk to, where they go and, controversially, in how they dress.

There are many myths associated with the crime of rape. We'll try to address some of these in this chapter, as well as relate to you the different types of rapist there are and the depths to which they will go to live out their perverse sexual thrills. We will also look at how the attainment of sexual thrills is ultimately not the aim of the rapist. For the rapist, the crime is all about power and control – the power to have a woman do what he says, without question or hesitation. Like the serial killer, he has the power of life and death in the palm of his hand – and this excites him beyond belief.

In the same way that there are myths about rape, there are also some hard facts. Perhaps the most chilling is this: rape is a very real threat for every female in the UK, no matter what age she might be. The Rape Crisis Federation for England and Wales estimates that out of around 48,000 calls it dealt with in 1998, only 12% of the woman involved had gone to the police. Also on average 1 in 4 women have suffered an attempted rape. So whilst the number of reported rapes in 1996 was 5,759, the real figure is likely to be much greater and there is no doubt that there is a high occurrence of the crime in this country. International crime surveys have consistently revealed that the UK has one of the highest rates of sexual assault in the world.

Contrary to popular belief, rape is not entirely a sexual act – rather it is an act of violence, power and control, which uses sex as a weapon. More sinister is the fact that for repeat sexual offenders rape can be a psychological progression toward even more extreme behaviours, most notably sexual homicide.

At the moment of impact, the rapist feels like he is the most potent being on earth. He needs to totally dominate another person, a weaker person, in order to compensate for his own inadequacies and low opinions of himself. He needs to feel special, and he achieves this in the most despicable way imaginable.

By using sex as a weapon, the rapist physically and psychologically destroys his victim. Their lives will never be the same again. The sexual pleasure is minimal, and sometimes the rapist does not achieve an erection and/or fails to ejaculate. Once the crime is committed, however, the rapist will relive the events over and over again in his mind, masturbating while he does so to achieve some form of sexual gratification.

When looking at the underlying psychological traits that make up a rapist, in order to try and explain why they commit such acts we must first look at their upbringing. In many ways, psychopathic sexual offenders are tarred with the same brush. Many of them come from a dysfunctional family background and many of them have been abused, both mentally and sexually. While the abuse inflicted upon them as children cannot be offered as a direct excuse for their acts in later life it does lead to one critical factor: they associate sex with being a weapon of domination and control. For these people, anything that gives them the chance to have some semblance of control – regardless of the violation of other people's rights – is something they must sample for themselves.

However, not every rapist has been sexually abused. For this minority, something deeper within compels them to rape. As we have already stated, a psychopath is someone who has no conscience or scruples. Their ultimate aim is to feel pleasure in whatever they do, no matter what the cost, physically, emotionally or even financially, to other people. We have also seen that the psychopath quite often does not feel that they are in full control of their destinies – they believe that society, the world around them, is to blame for their lot in life. As a result they feel a deep hatred and loathing for society, which in turn they want to destroy.

Psychopaths target the weakest members of society. While serial killers and rapists invariably target women and children, white-collar psychopaths such as fraudsters and conmen will look to the elderly to provide their kicks and monetary gain. Each of these victim types is more easily overpowered than men. That is not to say, however, that men are never raped. They are. We have come across a number of men who have been sexually assaulted. The fact that statistically there appear to be less male rape victims could be due to numerous sociocultural factors, such as the embarrassment of reporting a male-on-male rape, and the shame being a male rape victim brings.

No matter whether the victim is a woman or a man, we have to remember that for the psychopath sex is simply another weapon in their considerable arsenal which they utilise to derive pleasure. It allows them to feel in control of their destinies, helping them to believe that they are destroying a part of society they detest.

Anger and resentment, frustration with society, a seething internal rage, all combined with a low sense of self-esteem lead to the rapist using sex as a weapon.

Curiously, Australia has an unusually high instance of rape. For the purposes of this book, it is worth taking a moment to consider why this might be. Perhaps the patriarchal Australian society with its concept of machismo and male domination is to blame. Likewise, the country's historic past and its blatant maltreatment and disparaging attitude towards women could be a reason for the high instances of sexual assault.

In his international bestselling book, *The Fatal Shore*, author and art critic Robert Hughes has this to say about some of the 24,000 women that were transported to the antipodes between 1788 and 1852: 'Many Australians still think that their Founding Mothers were whores ...' Hughes continues this argument commentating that the colonial society took every opportunity to denegrate women convicts describing 'the degeneracy, incorrigibility and worthlessness of women convicts in Australia ...' The early women of Australia moved into the class of fiction becoming 'crude, raucous Eve, sucking rum and mothering bastards in the exterior darkness', setting the foundations for a potentially misogynistic society, something that is reflected in the statistics of sexual assault. Some writers have even gone so far as to describe Australia as one of the most misogynistic countries in the world. This misogyny is also derived from the emphasis upon aggression in the Australian male's upbringing, which is manifested in the type of sports that are so popular.

The above argument certainly seems appropriate when discussing the power assertive rapist (who we'll look at in more depth later in this chapter), but it fails to give a reason as to why other types of rapist elsewhere do what they do.

It supports the myth that rape is committed because men feel they have a right to have sex whenever, and with whoever, they want. In fact, as we've discussed earlier, we now know that rape is about power and control – it is not about satisfying a high libido.

Whatever your beliefs or thoughts on the reasons for why rape and sexual assault is commited, what cannot be dismissed are its devastating consequences and the effects the crime has on its victims. According to the International Association of Chiefs of Police, rape is 'one of the most serious violations of a person's body because it deprives the victim of both physical and emotional privacy and autonomy'.

Victims suffer emotionally and physically. The devastation experienced is difficult to conceptualise, let alone put into words. For a moment, try and imagine how it must feel to be a rape victim. Put yourself in their place for a short while.

You are lying asleep in your bed when a noise wakes you. You see a dark shape standing by the doorway, slowly walking towards you, with what looks like a knife in one hand. Before you can even think of screaming, the thing leaps onto the bed and you feel a hand clamp over your mouth and force your head down into the pillow. You're wide awake now. The terror is all consuming. In your mind you know that you could die at any moment. You know this because the thing, a man, wearing a black coat and balaclava, is holding a knife to your throat and its tip is pricking hard into your flesh. There is no sound in the room, save for your pulse throbbing in your temples and the rustle of the sheets as the man pulls them off the bed. Uncovered now, he rips off your nightdress. You can do nothing but obey him. All of your childhood nightmares have suddenly become real. The monster that as a child you feared is alive, about to violate you in every possible way, physically, psychologically, emotionally and spiritually.

How would you feel when the man left? How would you behave from that moment on? Do you think you would be the same person in the morning you were the night before? We have met and talked with rape victims whose lives have been radically altered by their experience. For many, their lives following their assault are spent trying to come to terms with what has happened. Their lives do change.

Paul Jacob who we met earlier when viewing the Granny Killer case, is a detective with the New South Wales Police Homicide and Serial Violent Crime Agency, and has worked on a number of major rape cases throughout the state in his 21-year career. On an almost daily basis, he comes into contact with the victims of serious sexual assaults such as rape.

'No matter how many times you see victims, you know that they have gone through a nightmare and that that nightmare will be with them forever,' Paul says.

'These women, and they are almost always women, have been violated in a horrible way,' he adds. 'When they report the offence they have to go through what for them is a humiliating physical examination but for us is a necessary and vital aspect of the case. Then, when the offender is caught and charged, they sometimes have to face him and identify him and then go through the whole ordeal in court before a packed room of strangers. I have nothing but immense respect and admiration for them and I am continually astounded at their spirit and fortitude.'

Quite often victims of rape will suffer depression, anxiety, have a lack of trust and become withdrawn. 'They are filled with a sense of shame and when they know the offender they have a greater sense of self-blame,' reveals Paul. 'Then there's the guilt, the humiliation, the anger, rage, betrayal and low sense of self-worth. They suffer horribly.'

The physical suffering is also intense. Victims suffer recurrent headaches, muscle tension, stomach upsets, sexually transmitted diseases, urinary tract complaints, and unwanted pregnancies. They are likely to consider committing suicide, often become dependent on drugs or alcohol, suffer insomnia, anorexia, nightmares, and develop phobias.

Sometimes the stigma attached to being a victim of a sexual assault, together with the disbelief of family and friends that the incident occurred, are other problems victims face and ones that potentially hinder their overall recovery.

So who are these men that rape? What are they like? How do they develop and how dangerous are they?

There are a number of different types of rapist and each is unique in terms of motivation and psychology. In the majority of instances the rapist is known to the victim – making a mockery of the myth that the rapist is usually a stranger. While both types of rape (stranger and known assailant) are about power and control, the stranger offender has more complex motivations behind his crime because of his different developmental experiences and the different level of emphasis placed on the act as a central factor within his life.

The image of the rapist as a stranger comes from the fact that these are the kinds of rapes that are reported in the media most often. More commonly the offender is a husband, friend, boyfriend or acquaintance of the victim. Recent crime figures show that in well over half of the cases of sexual assault reported, the victim knew the offender, with only a quarter stating that their attacker was a stranger. Date rape, where the victim and the offender are in, or have been in, some form of personal social relationship (ranging from a first date to an established relationship) is now one of the most common types of sexual assault.

This crime has received massive media publicity over the past decade, thanks in large part to the so-called date rape drug Rohypnol, which has emerged around the world's club scene and has already become established as a staple 'club drug'. Manufactured in the past by pharmaceutical company, Hoffman-La Roche, Rohypnol – which goes by a number of street names such as roofies, roachies, rope and rib, – is a brand name for Flunitrazepam, a high strength sedative and muscle relaxant which is said to be ten times more potent than Valium. In the UK, it is illegal to possess Rohypnol without a prescription and it is only available privately and not on the NHS.

Offenders have been known to covertly spike their victim's drink in order to incapacitate them, usually at a party, in a bar or at a club. The results are horrific. Within seconds the drug dissolves into the drink without trace*. Two or three small sips are then enough to ingest a hefty dosage. In 20 to 30 minutes, the brain's senses dull, commands from it to the central nervous system are reduced to almost nil, and the victim suffers a blackout that could last anywhere from between eight to 24 hours.

When the victim awakes, they are usually in unfamiliar surroundings with unfamiliar people, and have invariably been the victim of a sexual assault. The drug is so powerful however,

* As a result of the potential problems associated with it, and in order to combat sexual assaults linked to it: usage, Rohypnol's chemical make-up has been changed slightly. Today, when a Rohypnol tablet is dissolved in a liquid, it turns that liquid blue, thereby making it obvious that a tablet has been placed in the liquid. A precipitate has also been placed in the drug so that when it is dissolved, granules are left behind to further indicate its presence. While this is a positive development there are still many more prescription sedatives available illegally, which are being used by psychopaths to help them commit rape. This is a major cause of concern, and one that needs to be addressed, as we are all potential victims of this illegal drugs trade.

that at the moment they awake they have little or no memory of the act or acts that have been committed against their person. They attribute their headache, and situation, to their intake of alcohol the night before. It is only after a few days that they realise the awful truth of what has happened. It is at that moment, that for them the nightmare begins.

What kind of person commits this type of rape and how can you be protected? Unlike the four major types of stranger rapist, the date rapist can be divided into three fundamental subtypes depending upon motivational characteristics and the extent of the previous relationship with the victim. These are the 'intimate' date rapist, the 'acquaintance' date rapist and the 'stranger' date rapist.

The 'intimate' date rapist is someone who is or was in a relationship with the victim. This offender type quite often forces the victim to have sexual intercourse because there is a sense of entitlement. He wrongly believes that he has a right to have sex with his victim, by virtue of the fact that he has been steadily dating her for a period of time. He rationalises the rape by believing that what he has done could not possibly be considered wrong – after all, so he says, he and the victim are in love, and they would eventually have had sex anyway.

The 'acquaintance' date rapist is an individual who is known on a superficial level by the victim. He is probably a friend of a friend, for example. This offender will usually be slightly intoxicated at the time of the attack and with his lack of inhibitions, will be sexually aggressive. He is therefore more likely to force the victim to consent to intercourse. They feel they are entitled to sex. Maybe they have paid for an expensive meal, or have taken the victim to the opera. Whatever the event, the rapist believes sex is compensation for the money he has spent on the date, and at any rate, he knows the victim, she knows him, so forcing her to have sex is not really rape in his mind.

The 'stranger' date rapist is an individual who is likely to use drugs, alcohol or sedatives as a tool to control a victim. Typically, this type of rape is premeditated – the rapist has a plan to capture someone, takes the drugs or sedatives with him and hunts for a suitable victim.

The common thread between all of these rapists is that potential victims cannot detect who they are prior to an assault taking place. We believe that everyone, at some stage in their lives, has encountered one of the individuals we have just described – it is only by a stroke of luck or fortunate circumstances that many more people have not been attacked.

While date rapists are becoming increasingly common, by far more usual are the offenders we will talk of now – the power reassurance rapist, the power assertive rapist, the anger-hostility rapist and finally the anger-excitation rapist. They are sexual predators, a danger to anyone who comes across them. And there are many of them active at any one time.

The Power Reassurance Rapist
The most common and least physically dangerous stranger rapist , this type of sexual offender is sometimes referred to as the compensatory or gentleman rapist, on account of his 'unselfish' behaviour during the attack.

His main aim in committing the rapes is asserting power and control over a woman in order to prove to both himself and her that he is capable of being a sexually potent male well able to satisfy anyone. He is reassuring himself of his masculinity through demonstrating his power and control via sex.

This offender has a number of distinctive physical, verbal and sexual characteristics that he exhibits during the commission of the rape. These telltale traits allow us to enter his mind.

He is usually of above average intelligence, but possesses poor social skills when it comes to speaking with members of the opposite sex. His sexual experience will be limited and he will have had little, if any, experience in dating a woman. As a result, he fantasises about what could be – he dreams of having a woman to love, and spends much of his time fantasising about the things he would do sexually with a willing partner. These fantasies dominate his thoughts and he comes to believe in them, seeing himself as a super-male who women are incredibly attracted to and want to have sex with.

The power reassurance rapist is a loner and may not fit in socially. They may well have been abused as children, and almost certainly were shown no love by their parents. As a result they have probably always felt isolated and withdrawn – feelings which will have bred resentment over time.

Like many other forms of psychopathy they create fantasy worlds in which they are loved, recognised and accepted by their victims. They crave this recognition as a special person, yet in the real world, these inadequate individuals are shunned, shattering their sense of self-worth.

Great actors, these individuals know how to fit in – they

mimic acceptable behaviour on a daily basis. As a result they feel more superior to everyone else, living an incredible lie of their own making – one that fools the whole of society.

Their development into a full-blown rapist will usually come about following a period of voyeurism, which often will have begun by chance. Walking home late at night they might see a woman getting undressed in her bedroom. They will watch her for a while, growing excited by their secret observations. Very quickly they will turn this chance occurrence into more regular behaviour. They will fantasise about various aspects of what they see on their prowls, deriving additional sexual pleasure from their nocturnal habits as they do so.

Eventually they will become bored with their sexual fantasies of voyeurism and want more from their peeping sessions. They will shift their focus from merely watching a woman undressing to actually being there with her in the flesh. However, they know that this is unlikely to happen, as they do not possess the necessary social skills to be able to get close enough to a woman. The only way they can do this is to force the woman to be with them. Very quickly, their thoughts turn to rape.

During the attack, the rapist acts in a way he believes is pleasing to his victim – hence the gentleman label. He believes he is a superb and virile lover who the woman wants and may well fall in love with. As a result, he will commit the kind of sex acts on the victim that he believes women ultimately want. Cunnilingus, as well as digital stimulation of the vagina before actual penetration, are often a trademark of this rapist. The woman beneath him is not a victim. Rather, in his mind, she is a willing partner in an intimate act of love.

In almost all instances he will have rehearsed words and phrases – a kind of script – which he will use during the attack. These phrases, such as 'tell me how good I am' and 'tell me you love me and want me', enable him to rationalise his behaviour as being normal and lead him to believe that the woman is enjoying the experience.

Generally this rapist will attack a victim who is close to him in age, and usually late at night. He will not go out of his way to inflict pain and terror on his victim, but may well do so over time, as his search for a soul mate proves fruitless.

Incredibly, and what serves as an interesting pointer to this offender's mental instability, he may contact the victim following the rape in an attempt to continue the relationship he has built up in his mind. It has even been known for this rapist to send his victim flowers, chocolates and other gifts as tokens of his love days after the rape has occurred.

The Power Assertive Rapist

This is a man who has no doubts about who or what he is. He is a macho man, a real male. When he rapes a person, he is simply exercising what he feels is his right to have sex with whatever woman he chooses. As a member of the stronger sex, he believes that he should be able to do whatever he wants with a woman. If she resists, she is questioning his masculinity and should be punished.

Unlike the power reassurance rapist, there is very little of the fantasy aspect about the rape displayed by this form of predator. He is more impulsive and spontaneous. When the time is right and a woman makes herself available he will use his charming and manipulative social skills to get close to her, have her believe she is safe and then attack her.

There are no thoughts about making the experience of rape 'pleasurable' for the woman with this rapist. In all aspects, this man is selfish – verbally, physically and sexually. He gets what he wants, which is to have the woman submit completely to his every desire.

His attack is violent. He will rip the clothes off his victim's body and may well subject the woman to repeated sexual assaults as a further sign of his supreme manhood.

This offender is driven by the need to have his victim completely under his control. This is where the real thrill comes from for him. For it all to work properly in his mind, he must show the woman who is the boss – who is the strongest. He will do this by humiliating her in any manner he sees fit.

Quite often when looking at psychopaths and their crimes, the behavioural patterns they exhibit during the commission of their offences are also evidenced in their home life. In this case the power assertive rapist is likely to treat his wife or partner badly – he will be the dominant partner and will neglect his children (if he has any), believing that raising them is a job fit only for a woman. Socially he will be outgoing and physical – playing contact sports or engaging in what he sees as masculine.

The Anger-Hostility Rapist

With this rapist we enter a new level of psychology, far from that of the first two offenders described.

The anger-hostility rapist has a pathological hatred of women. The frustration they experience in life is usually attributed to a female, and the rapes committed by this offender are ways in which to relieve the anger they have which threatens to overpower them psychologically. In plain English, they are getting even with the female race for real or imagined wrongs done against them.

They view women as sexual objects – simple whores with no feelings or opinions that are worth a passing thought. To get back at such a being as this is easy – you destroy her through sex.

Sickeningly, this offender often goes beyond inflicting himself sexually on his victim. In some cases he will attempt to permanently erase the identity of the woman concerned by attacking her genitalia – something he hopes will serve as a traumatic reminder of what happened, with the aim of causing as much psychological pain as possible.

The actual attack is an intense emotional outburst, which is usually triggered by something said or done by a woman associated with the rapist in some way. A blitz-style of attack is the method commonly used when capturing a victim, giving her no opportunity to resist. When he has his victim under control, he will rape her repeatedly and humiliate her throughout the assault, both by words and actions. He may also beat her severely in his desire to obliterate her identity completely, and will more than likely be armed with a knife or similar weapon, which he will brandish quite openly and use freely to terrorise the victim.

The Anger-Excitation Rapist

This type of offender is also called the sadistic rapist, which is certainly a more definitive way to describe him, for he is sadistic in every sense of the word and without doubt the most brutal of all rapists. In fact, this type of rapist is very closely related to the serial killer and it is not uncommon for these psychopaths to progress to murder.

The anger-excitation rapist associates aggression and suffering with sexual arousal. The more pain and suffering there is, the more aggressive they become – and the more aggressive they become, the more sexually aroused they are. Reading between the lines, it's not hard to understand the reasons for them inflicting even greater levels of torture and pain on their victims, as they are inclined to do. In many cases, the rape and pain only ends with the offender's orgasm – or the victim's death.

The sadistic rapist plans his crimes extensively. He is intelligent and meticulous in his preparations, reading up on police investigative procedures and the like. There is probably one such individual reading this book right now. He will collect weapons and take the time to learn how to build torture devices and even soundproof rooms. He will usually stalk his victims, biding his time until the moment comes when he feels it is right to strike.

The attack itself will be brutal. The aim is to inflict as much pain and damage as possible to ensure that the victim is under his complete control. Whips, chains, knives, scalpels, garrottes, blindfolds and gags may all be called into use during the rape.

He will use these tools to inflict incredible beatings and abuse on his unfortunate victims. It is not unusual for a victim to have her nipples bitten or cut off during the assault or to be strangled to the point of unconsciousness only to be brought back from the brink of death time and again so as to prolong the attack.

The rape may also be recorded either on video or audio cassette. These are then used post-offence by the rapist to relive the attack and experience again the highs of sexual pleasure it brought.

One rape is not enough for this offender. Indeed, for these individuals, no rape is ever going to be as good as their fantasies. Hence the reason for repeat – serial – rapes. They are always looking for ways to improve their attack and perfect their fantasies, resulting in them hunting again and again. They will never stop offending. They will eventually kill. They are among the most dangerous and formidable human predators that we know of.

Opportunistic Rapist

This is the only rapist who rapes primarily for sex. Usually this offender rapes when an opportunity presents itself during the commission of another crime, such as a burglary, kidnapping or robbery. For example, a man may accost a woman in a dark street with the sole intention of stealing her purse. She may well be drunk and offer little resistance and he may find her sexually attractive and go on to rape as well as rob her.

The reason for this attack is not to experience power, control and domination. Quite clearly, it is an afterthought, the seizing of a momentary chance to attain sexual pleasure.

While on paper the differences between the types of rapist are clear, in the real world when a rapist strikes, it is often hard for investigators and the public in general to understand who and what it is they are dealing with.

The following case history is that of one of the most famous rape cases criminal history. It offers a chilling glimpse inside the real world of a combined power assertive/power reassurance rapist. It is an excellent example of how one particular offender does not fit perfectly into one specific typology or classification.

The Blacktown Rapist

Blacktown is located roughly 30 km west of Sydney, Australia. Although large in comparison to many of the country's suburbs, it is relatively unknown outside of the Sydney area. But in the early 1970s, the spotlight was firmly focused on it, for all the wrong reasons.

For seven months between December 1972 and July 1973, Blacktown was the hunting ground for a brazen and terrifying serial rapist. In total four women were raped, one other was seriously sexually assaulted, and the offender committed a plethora of other related offences, including a number of burglaries, and was also responsible for a number of peeping tom incidents in the area, both prior to and during the series of rapes.

A young Blacktown housewife, sleeping alone in her bed, was victim number one. The date was 10 December, 1972, a balmy summer's evening. A cruel quirk of fate had led to the woman being alone that night. Along with her husband, she had been invited to a neighbour's Christmas party, but having spent the day battling the crowds hunting for suitable presents, she was tired and decided not to go to the party. She insisted that her husband should attend, despite his protests, and when he eventually left for the party, she made herself a cup of hot chocolate and went to bed, leaving the back door unlocked and the kitchen and front porch lights switched on.

Music from the party next door filtered through to her, providing a false sense of security. Eventually at about 11 pm, she dozed off. She awoke at 3 am feeling something soft being placed over her head. She struggled awake and sensed the dark shape of a man leaning over her, holding what looked and felt like a blanket, which he was wrapping around her head. She screamed. The man dropped the blanket and ran out of the room. Awake now, and thinking that the man was her husband returning drunk from the party, she unwrapped the blanket from around herself and walked cautiously to the bedroom door. Peering into the hallway, she saw the outline of the man switching off the lights at the rear of the house.

Panicked, she ran back to the bed and in what would prove to be a futile act, got under the covers, pulled them over herself and waited, paralysed with fear, her breath caught in her throat. A few minutes later the man returned. This time he was armed with a kitchen knife and once next to the bed, ripped the covers off the terrified woman. Her loud screams failed to unnerve him. Calmly he leant towards her with the knife and said that if she didn't stop screaming he would kill her.

What followed was a vicious assault, during which the woman was raped, fondled, and forced to perform various sexual acts, while the rapist held the knife to her throat. She was physically hurt, with the stranger savagely biting one of her breasts.

With the rape over, the offender ransacked the house looking for cash and valuables. The speed and skill with which the offender stole goods from the house suggested to detectives attending the scene that their suspect was an accomplished burglar who had progressed to a more violent crime.

A little over a week later, the woman received another shock. The rapist telephoned her. Not once, but repeatedly. During his final call to her, he called her by her name and then threatened to return and rape her again soon. Within a matter of a couple of weeks, the woman and her husband had left their home and moved out of the area, never to return.

A young mother, sleeping with her two-year-old daughter while her husband worked a night shift, was the rapist's next victim, exactly three weeks later. This attack was less than a kilometre from the first one, suggesting that the suspect knew the area well and possibly either lived or worked in the vicinity.

Victim number two was awoken at 3 am with a pair of icy-cold hands fondling her body. Coming out of her slumber, she sensed her arms being lifted above her head, then felt the weight of a man sitting on her chest, demanding in a deep voice that she perform oral sex on his erect penis.

She screamed, but quickly stopped when the man threatened to stab her if she didn't. She then began to sob. Her sobs awoke her daughter, who began to call for her mother from the other side of the bed. Without a hint of panic, the suspect allowed the woman to soothe and comfort her child until the toddler fell back to sleep. With the child now quiet, he raped the woman repeatedly, subjecting her to an hour-long assault, performing numerous acts on her.

Once again, when the rape was over, he calmly got up, dressed himself and ransacked the house, before leaving as silently and stealthily as he had arrived. However, unlike at the first rape scene, this time he left something behind – a set of murky fingerprints on a toolbox he had obviously contemplated stealing. It was a small break for the police.

The wife of a police detective had a lucky escape two weeks later, when the Blacktown Rapist, as he was now called, struck again in the early hours of January 15. The woman was watching TV when she heard footsteps coming from her bedroom upstairs. She knew it couldn't be her husband, as he was on a night shift at one of the nearby police stations. Grabbing a bottle of gin as a weapon, she quietly made her way upstairs to investigate the source of the noise. Entering the bedroom and turning on the light, she was confronted by the sight of man leaping towards her, his hands outstretched.

Grabbing her, the suspect held her in a headlock and put his free hand over the woman's mouth. The family dog, locked in another room, began to bark at the noise. The dog's barking woke the woman's sleeping baby. The baby's cries infuriated the suspect, who dragged the woman back into the bedroom and threatened to kill her if she made any noise. A scuffle ensued during which the woman was able to bite and hold in her mouth three of the rapist's fingers. She held on for dear life, while the man struggled to break free. Somehow he managed to extract himself, barged past the woman and fled through the bedroom window.

The woman called police, who rushed to the scene, scoured the streets and found nothing. Ten days later, the woman's home telephone rang. When she answered, she heard what sounded like a youngish man say that he might have failed the first time, but that he'd 'rape you the next time you're alone'.

Victim number four was not so lucky. The offender grabbed the pregnant woman from behind as she put down her kitchen telephone, following a conversation with her mother. This time the suspect was wearing a white mask, concealing his face, but like the other attacks he was again armed with a knife, with which he threatened to kill the victim if she resisted him or made a noise.

She was dragged to her upstairs bedroom, stripped of her clothes and raped repeatedly. When the offender had had enough, he dressed himself and again ransacked the house looking for money and other valuable possessions.

When police arrived on the scene, they got lucky. In his rush to escape, the offender had dropped a set of keys, which included two Holden car keys, a locker key and a front door key. Hairs belonging to the suspect were also found on the victim's bed and the suspect's fingerprint was found on the doorknob of the laundry door.

Once again, illustrating a pattern of behaviour for which it is hard to find an explanation, the Blacktown Rapist telephoned his latest victim and threatened her. The woman slammed down the phone and ran out of the house screaming. The following day, while she sought sanctuary with her parents, her husband packed all their belongings, locked the front door to the house and together they walked away, never to set foot in the house or the street again.

The Blacktown Rapist's fifth and final victim was attacked two months later on April 26. The attack was just as vicious as all the others. It occurred in the early hours of the morning, and uncannily the victim was also sharing her bed with her daughter while her husband worked a night shift. The woman was raped repeatedly and when the attack was over, a number of her possessions were stolen. However, prior to the rape taking place the victim had tried to have a conversation with the slim, long, dark-haired suspect and had asked his name. The suspect replied that she could call him Peter.

This time the police got a substantial number of fingerprints, as well as a palm-print, which they were able to match positively with other prints found at previous crime scenes. A call from a former police officer also proved vital in finally nailing the suspect. One of the items stolen following the second rape was a .303 rifle complete with a telescopic sight. According to the former police officer, his son knew someone who fitted the description of the rapist and had been boasting about owning a .303 rifle with telescopic sight. According to the ex-officer, the person in question was called Peter and had long, dark hair.

It transpired that the Blacktown Rapist was employed by the Water Board and lived with his widowed mother and brother in the Blacktown area. He was an accomplished burglar and prowler, and had committed his first theft at the age of 13. In his interview with the police immediately after his arrest, the Blacktown Rapist had this to say about how he chose his victims: 'I would just wander about the streets looking for a home with a single light glowing from inside. Then I would check the driveway. If the car was missing, I regarded it as a sure sign that either the house was empty or the woman was alone inside.'

When questioned about the level of violence he had used during his attacks and his threats to the victims afterwards, he said it was all bluff.

'If they gave me a hard time, I was prepared to leave without actually stabbing anyone,' he said.

The judge presiding over the case failed to believe him and the Blacktown Rapist was sentenced to 20 years in jail.

Shannon

No matter which type of rapist a victim is attacked by, the results are inevitably the same – a victim who is left devastated mentally and physically by the assault, whose life is never the same again.

Shannon is 33, but she will be the first to tell you that she looks much older. Eight years ago she was sexually assaulted. The man who attacked her has never been caught. She did not report the matter to the police, fearing that her story would not be believed. We have included it here, as we believe the assault did take place and that Shannon was a victim of the date rape drug Rohypnol, given to her by a psychopath bent on sexual pleasure.

Every Thursday through to Sunday night I used to work at a popular bar. It was always busy, and I knew most of the regulars that drank there. It was always a fun place. I loved working there, it was a release for me and I enjoyed being part of a large crowd of young, fun and trendy people.

Sometimes after my shift finished on a Saturday night, I'd

touch up my make-up and head off with friends and hang out at a couple of the nightclubs. I loved the scene, the music, the dressing up, meeting new people. I used to really look forward to it. I would always be the one who wanted to keep on partying no matter how late it was. Once I was on the dance-floor feeling the beat of the music, I was in heaven and never wanted it to stop. I lived for those nights and used to look forward to them so much.

I would go to the clubs with a group of anywhere between five and eight people. There was an equal mix of men and women; most of them were in relationships. At the time I was 24 and single. One of the guys who would come with us now and again was called Brent. I had always got on well with him. He was a labourer. I liked him, fancied him a bit, but knew that he had a girlfriend in Perth so I never said anything about my feelings for him. We remained good friends, part of the same crowd.

One Sunday night, Brent came into the bar. He was with a couple of his mates, from work I think, and he spent the whole night watching me and smiling. Every time I'd glance over to where he was sitting I'd be met with his smile. I realised he was flirting with me and went along with it, smiling at him and making sure that I was available to serve him whenever he came to the bar to buy another drink.

We eventually got a chance to talk to one another about 30 to 40 minutes before the bar closed. It was quiet, so the manager let me finish early and have a drink with Brent. I poured myself a drink, a coke with ice, and we sat down and began chatting. Brent told me that his girlfriend had left him a couple of weeks previously and that he was a bit depressed. I felt sorry for him and decided to let him talk, as he seemed to want to get it off his chest.

After about 15 minutes, he asked me if I wanted a drink, a 'proper drink' as he called it. I said no at first, but he pleaded with me to have one more drink with him, so I thought what the hell, why not? He went to the bar while I had a cigarette. A minute or so later, he came back with a double rum and pineapple juice with ice for me and a schooner of beer for himself and we sat down and began talking again.

I remember feeling ill about an hour later. I remember the room spinning and my head feeling thick and cloudy, and I remember Brent holding me by the arm as we walked. I'd taken some Ecstasy the night before, and initially I thought it was the drug still in my system and that the combination of it with the rum, was making me lose my senses and feel sick.

I remember nothing of what was said, what happened next, or where we went. What occurred in the next nine or 10 hours I have no clear recollection of exactly, but I can guess.

At some stage in the evening I remember lying on my back on top of a bed, with a red and black striped duvet. I was naked and cold. The shivering brought me around, I think. A man was kneeling between my legs inserting his erect penis into me. I think I was moaning, I am sure I was saying no, but I can't remember clearly. All I can remember is him saying something to me, encouraging me, kissing me and then pushing himself into me and squeezing my breasts.

I woke up at 10.30 the following morning. My vagina was raw and sore and stung to the touch. Brent was lying asleep naked next to me.

I was astonished to be there. I had no real idea where I was, how I'd got there, or what had happened during the night to have me wake up in the state I was in. I had an excruciating headache, felt horribly hung-over yet could only recall having had one drink. I began to panic. I started shaking Brent, trying to wake him up.

He said nothing to me, except, 'Get dressed'. I'll never forget the look on his face when he said the words. I began to cry. I asked him to tell me what had gone on. He told me that I'd come on to him at the pub and begged him to sleep with me. He said we'd had a good time, but that now I had to go. At no stage in my life had I ever gone home with a guy on the first night before this. It was completely out of character for me. I would never willingly give myself sexually to someone unless I knew them very well, cared for them and loved them, and believed they felt the same way about me.

I know that he raped me. I have lived through the nightmare of what happened to me everyday. I have asked myself time and time again, what kind of man would do such a thing to me. I have never been able to find an answer.

I used to be a flirt. I used to enjoy dressing up in revealing clothes and showing off my body. I was proud of the way I looked and I had always wanted to be a model. I had made no secret of the fact that I fancied Brent. I felt that if I told people, the police, my friends, about what I thought had happened, none of them would believe me and I would have been shunned. I kept my mouth shut and have lived with the regret ever since.

I no longer go to bars. I no longer go to clubs. I no longer flirt with men. I no longer wear the kinds of clothes I want to. Today I don't trust men. I have not had a relationship with anybody for almost eight years and I don't think I will ever have one again.

I'm trying to put my life back in order, but am finding it hard to do so. I have a good career now in design and have just bought my own flat. I am lonely. I am often depressed. I find it difficult to sleep at nights. I often wonder why I am alive, and for what purpose. I think about him and hope that he is having a miserable time, although I suspect he probably isn't. I wonder how many other women he has raped. I wonder if any of them have been strong enough to tell the truth about what happened to them. I pray that there is one out there. I feel ashamed that I am not her.

CHAPTER 5

Suffer The Children

Serial killers, stalkers, serial rapists, white collar psychopaths. Their crimes are despicable, often unexplainable and without fail, shocking in the extreme. But the public's revulsion at such offences is nothing compared to those committed by one type of offender – the child killer. The needless slaughter of society's true innocents – the Hollys, the Jessicas, the Millys, the Jamies, the Ainlees – is more than most of us can bear. It is these deaths, more than others, these seemingly unexplainable and wanton acts of all too often premeditated violence, that shock us to the core and have us collectively asking the same time-old question: why?

The answer to that question is, unfortunately, disturbingly easy to answer. We know the fundamental psychological drivers of the psychopath's behaviour. We know that in the vast majority of cases they choose their victims randomly. We also know that in all cases they are merciless. More importantly, and this is the key, we know that these types of individuals prey on those who they see as being vulnerable and weak. Victims they can dominate and control easily. The easily frightened. And there are no more weaker or vulnerable potential victims than children. Our children are no longer safe – as a glance through newspapers around the world will prove – and more and more of them are falling victim to psychopaths than ever before.

While cases such as that involving 10-year-olds Holly Wells and Jessica Chapman are guaranteed to dominate headlines and receive maximum public exposure, there are many more children murdered each year in the United Kingdom than we would perhaps like to imagine. And what is even more shocking is the fact that these children are often murdered by the very people with whom they should feel safest – their parents.

'Any child killing is a shocking and tragic event,' says Mary Marsh, the director of the NSPCC. 'But what is even more disturbing is the fact that a child is more likely to be murdered in the home than on the street. In fact, every year around 80 children are killed in the home in England and Wales alone by the very people who should protect them from danger – the child's parents and carers. This is a national disgrace.'

While domestic child abuse often goes unnoticed, recent headline making cases, such as that of two-year-old Ainlee Walker have highlighted the risks all our children, from all walks of life, face whether they are in or out of the home. But despite this, despite these staggering statistics, the cases that strike fear into every responsible parent in the country are those where the child's killer is a stranger. These murders, while only representing a small percentage of unlawful children's deaths, are a cruel reality of the world in which we live. And while many more children will be killed by psychopathic predators in the months and years to come, there is more we can do to keep our children safe. However, before we can do that, we need to understand what makes such offenders tick. Only then can we address the problem.

Before we do that, it is important to point out the difference between child killers and paedophiles as they are not one and the same. To begin with, we will look at paedophilia, what exactly it is, and the psychological and behavioural characteristics of paedophiles in a bid to understand perhaps one of the most sickening of all criminals.

According to the American Psychological Society's Diagnostic and Statistical Manual of Mental Disorders (Fourth Edition), paedophilia is 'the recurrent, intense presence of sexual urges and fantasies of at least six months' duration involving sexual activity with prepubescent children (this encompasses children aged 13 or younger)'.

Paedophilia is a subcategory of a larger group of sexual disorders commonly classified as paraphilias (a preference for or addiction to unusual sexual practices). These are defined as recurrent and intense aphrodisiac fantasies, sexual urges or behaviours over a prolonged period, which can involve non-human objects, the suffering or humiliation of oneself or one's partner, as well as children and other non-consenting partners.

There is a misconception that paedophilia only occurs when a child is touched. This is wrong, as paedophilia encompasses everything from voyeurism of nude or partially dressed children, to sexual fondling, the offender exposing himself to the child, and the performing or request of oral sex from the child. In most cases, except those involving incest, paedophiles do not require sexual penetration and do not force themselves on the child – because they don't have to. It is this cunning and manipulative aspect of their behaviour that highlights this offender's psychopathic characteristics. For, like the serial killer and rapist, the paedophile uses charm, guile, persuasion, tenderness and above all, his brain, to get what he wants. He will select his victim carefully and then win their trust, as well as the trust of their parents or friends, to generate and maintain contact with them. Like the stalker, he will shower his potential victim with kind words and sentiments, as well as gifts, all aimed at breaking down the barriers and allowing him to inflict himself on his unsuspecting victim.

And like all the other vicious psychopaths we have encountered, the paedophile justifies his actions – he rarely feels remorse – by claiming in almost all cases that it was the victim's fault that the molestation took place, it was they who solicited sexual contact, and that the child derived as much sexual pleasure from the activity as the offender did himself. And the paedophile will go even further than that in justifying and defending his actions. They will excuse their behaviour as non-harmful, non-violent, non-forced and, incredibly, even educational for the child concerned. They very often tend not to see themselves as abusers, molesters or sexual deviants. As clinicians, this denial, this sickening justification for what are always brutal acts, tells us a lot about the paedophile. It shows us, that just like their murderous cousins, paedophiles act with their own interests at heart. They are not overwhelmed by thoughts they can't control, nor are they driven by voices in their heads. They do what they do because it pleases them and purely and simply for their own personal gratification. The victim doesn't matter. It is the offender's self interests that are most important.

It is important to consider the fact that there are two types of paedophilic offender – the situational child molester and the preferential child molester. The first type of paedophile, somewhat like the disorganised serial killer, does not necessarily plan his attacks in great detail and depth. His crime is one of happenchance. He does not possess a genuine sexual preference for children – his motivators are purely criminal, they are not about fulfilling a latent sexual urge or desire. They are simply his way of getting back at society and all the perceived wrongs that society has dealt the offender. In some cases the situational child molester's sexual abuse of children is a broadening of other forms of abuse in his life. This continuum of anti-social behaviour could stem from his mistreatment of others, such as his spouse, friends, work colleagues or even adult strangers. This type of offender, like many other offenders before him, will have a low-self esteem, have minimal moral standards and consider sex with children as just another form of exerting his power and control over someone weaker and more vulnerable than him. Having a propensity for violence and anti-social behaviour is nothing new to this type of individual, and he will justify his sexual assaults on children as being merely a stepping stone in his out of control criminal career. Indeed, there are times when this individual sees children as a substitute for an adult partner. These offenders are aware of their inadequacies in forming genuine relationships with people of their own age and this factor, combined with their acute lack of social skills, pushes them towards children, who they see as being easy targets who are not only available but are more easily conned and flattered. The situational child molester will usually have very few victims and sometimes only one, and may never repeat the offence again.

The preferential child molester, on the other hand, is a much more systematic and deviant offender. This is the classic paedophile, a person who has a definite sexual preference for children and has usually had such a characteristic for most of his life. There are four major behavioural markers that set this offender apart from the situational child molester. Unlike the previous offender, the preferential child molester is someone who has exhibited a long-term and persistent pattern of such behaviour; children are his preferred sex objects; they have well-developed techniques in obtaining victims; and their sexual fantasies are solely focused on children. Studies have shown that like other serial sex offenders, many preferential child molesters have themselves been the victims of child sexual abuse. They will also have been arrested and charged with child molestation and abuse offences in the past, and will also have been arrested for non-sexual offences such as impersonating a police officer and theft. These offenders are committed to their cause, and will make repeated high-risk attempts to obtain children. These snatch and grab raids will have been meticulously thought out and, as has been seen all too frequently, will be carried out with both cunning and skill.

One of the prime behavioural traits of this type of paedophile is his ability to locate and acquire children almost at will. Some paedophiles can watch a group of children for a brief period of time and then select a potential target who, more often than not, is from a broken home or has been the victim of emotional and physical neglect. He will also work tirelessly on refining his technique to capture children. He will not simply stand outside a school and wait for the right child to walk into his arms. He will instead use all his persuasive charm, guile and manipulative skills to get near to his victim, make them feel safe and secure and then when the bond between potential victim and would-be offender has been sealed, he will strike. Quite often the paedophile will employ the same techniques of manipulation on the parents of his potential victims. This is a vital component of his hunting strategy. He needs a child that is either allowed to be with him (soccer coach, scout leader etc) or does not have a vigilant guardian. This tells us that the preferential child molester is fully aware of what he is doing and is in complete charge of his thoughts at the time of the crime. He knows that he must be charming and non-offensive when first approaching his intended victim – threats and violence can come later when the victim has been moved away from the scene of his abduction and the offender can exert complete control in a place where he is completely comfortable.

There are many more similarities between the psychological characteristics of the paedophile and the other psychopathic offenders we have so far seen in this book. For example, it is not unusual to discover that the paedophile will almost always have a wife or partner who is either a strong and domineering or weak and passive woman. Whatever characteristics this type of offender's significant other possesses, they will have one thing in common and that will be a lack of interest in sex – brought about by their husbands' lack of interest in them sexually and his inability to form a normal loving, adult sexual relationship. The paedophile will sometimes use his partner as a cover for his activities – she provides him with a level of respectability and can unwittingly help him get near to children, particularly if she already has children from a previous relationship. This cunning and manipulative streak, as we have already learnt, is a key behavioural and psychological characteristic of the psychopath. Like the serial killer, the paedophile will be very particular in the selection of his victims and will very quickly settle on a particular type of child on which to prey. It is common for active paedophiles to concentrate their attentions on children of a certain age and sex, although young girls are twice as more likely to be attacked than boys. The older the age preference of the paedophile, the more exclusive the gender preference. For example, offenders attracted to toddlers are more likely to molest boys and girls indiscriminately. A paedophile attracted to teenagers, however, will be very select about which gender he chooses. Another key factor to highlight is the fact that the preference age bracket will also differ between different paedophiles. Like serial killers, these offenders do not prey on the same type, age and gender of victim. It is more about how the potential victim looks, than how old they are. And once they find a 'fit' they very rarely, if at all, deviate from that set type of victim.

Paedophiles have been the subject of numerous medical, psychological, sociological and academic studies over the past 30 years, with the majority of these studies concerned with uncovering the reasons why these individuals engage in sexual activity with children.

It has been noted in such studies that paedophiles describe themselves as introverted, shy, sensitive and depressed. Objective personality tests, usually conducted when the paedophile is in prison, confirm these self-assessments but add to the overall picture such traits as emotional immaturity and a fear of being able to function in a mature heterosexual relationship. Another common characteristic of paedophiles, and one worthy of note, is a moralistic attitude towards sex and a sexual repression. There are presently two major medical and psychological ways employed to assess and diagnose paedophilia. Both of them are controversial and in our opinion not conclusive. The first is through phallometric testing (also referred to as penile plethysmorgraphic assessment, or PPG), which measures changes in the level of blood in the paedophile's penis while the offender is shown various erotic stimuli. The controversy surrounding this test is twofold. Firstly, the reliability of this test is difficult to confirm as physiological changes are easier to measure than interpret, and secondly, the offender's arousal may be a function of general arousability as opposed to the presence of any stimuli. To address these concerns, researchers have devised a second diagnostic tool as a central arousability system intended to work in-sync with the PPG. The so-called contingent negative variation (CNV) system measures brain wave activity as an index of sexual desire under conditions of sexual stimulation relevant to the paedophilic mindset.

Whether these systems are of benefit, either to society or the offender, remains to be seen, but we are of the opinion that such treatments cannot work. Why? Our answer is simple. Paedophiles do not believe that what they have done is harmful. This denial serves to assuage any guilt and therefore it is almost impossible to say whether a paedophile expressing remorse and sorrow over his actions can ever be truly believed or rehabilitated.

More worryingly perhaps is the massive growth of the Internet and the marked proliferation of child pornographic material on the world-wide web which provides the would-be paedophile (as well convicted and released paedophiles) with a private and world of children to abuse. In a 1998 Interpol raid a total of 500,000 pornographic images of children ranging in ages from two months to 16 years of age were found in the United States alone. Unfortunately this is just the tip of a very large iceberg. According to one study, as much as 45 percent of child pornography on the Internet originates in Japan where child pornography is not an offence. The FBI's Operation Candyman has recently made headlines around the world in the size and scale of its catch. The FBI campaign was named after an Internet group of over 7000 members, including priests, former police officers, teachers and doctors, ranging in age from 17 to 70, that was formed to help paedophiles upload and download child porn images. The site boasted that it was 'for people who love kids. You can post any type of message you like, and post any type of pics and vids'. It is sites like this that make the fight against paedophiles one of the most challenging and significant for law enforcement agencies around the world, and is something that all of us should be concerned about.

James

James didn't want to be interviewed. When I'd first approached him with the idea of an interview he told me that his reluctance to speak was purely because he didn't like to dwell on the past and didn't want to relive the years of pain and torment. He sounded like a victim. The classic victim, even. Sad, weary, grieving over some injustice. But James is anything but, and I knew that if I kept on badgering him and appealed to his sense of ego and flattered him enough, I would get him to speak. And speak he did. For James is a convicted paedophile, a 39-year-old man with a long criminal history. He is perhaps one of the most disturbing men I have ever met. And like all psychopaths he likes to talk about his moments of glory, those times when he was firmly in control of the world around him. I will long remember our time together. Having talked to him about his crimes, and listened to him methodically and intelligently justify his actions, I can only imagine the hell his victims must now be living through.

At first glance there is nothing untoward about James. He looks like any other relatively successful and well-balanced middle-class man. Indeed, if you were to judge him on his looks and first impressions alone, then you would perhaps say that he was a charming, honest and spiritually aware individual, who probably wouldn't hurt a fly. He is polite, softly-spoken, articulate and, outwardly at least, confident. It is no wonder that for almost a decade, his crimes went unsuspected and his victims kept their vows of silence.

In many ways James is the classic psychopath. It is very easy to use the word 'psychopath' glibly without understanding its true, clinical meaning. But in this case, the use of the word to describe who and what James is (regardless of his criminal past) is perfect. James is a psychopath. He even admits it himself.

'I have always known that I was different,' he said. 'I've never had a respect for the laws of society and I have never wanted to fit in. I can play the part of being a normal person and I do that everyday, but deep down I really don't care about people. I have my reasons for having done what I have done. I can't help what has happened. I have tried to feel remorseful, I have tried to feel sorry, but the truth is, I am not sorry for what has gone on. I am ashamed of my actions and who I am, but I am not sorry. And I never will be.'

James' criminal career began at the age of 11 when he started stealing chocolate bars and packets of crisps from his local corner shop. At the time he was playing truant from school, not because he disliked the educational system and possessed a rebellious spirit, but because he wanted to escape the classroom bullies who made his life hell.

'I was bullied at school, everyday,' he told me. 'What was worse was that I was bullied by girls. Older girls. It was because of the way I looked. I was an ugly child, I had no confidence in myself and those girls picked up on this and made my life a misery.'

He says that the reason he started stealing was simple – to gain respect. The more he stole, the less he was bullied. It's a classic excuse for wrongdoing. James exonerates his actions of the past by blaming others for his faults and like many other psychopaths we have met, he doesn't like having this pointed out to him.

'I knew I had a choice. I could either stay as I was and allow myself to be bullied by a bunch of idiots, or I could prove myself to them and be like them. And that's what I did. I picked their path and made my life easier.'

For four years James' criminal activity was entirely focused on shoplifting and he graduated from ripping off the local shop to targeting nearby shopping malls, where he stole everything from tape cassettes to bed linen, all of which he later sold.

'I used to get taxis to the shopping centres with the money I was making,' he boasted. 'I'd tell the driver to pick me up in 30 minutes and I'd load up the boot with whatever I'd nicked. Usually the drivers would help me sell the stuff. They [the taxi drivers] were all in on it. It was easy money.'

His hopes of winning the respect of the schoolyard bullies were short-lived, however. They continued to torment him, and their attitude towards him gradually worsened as they became aware of his vain attempts to seek their acceptance. As a result, James began to seek out ways in which he could gain revenge over them – through rape.

Analysing this for a moment, it is clear that it is at this point in James' developmental history that he first began nurturing deviant sexual thoughts about teenage girls. It is the start of his feelings of being ostracised by society – the onset of what clinicians label the offender's Negative Social Attachment, or his feelings or views that he is not wanted by society and is not valued by the people around him. This feeling of isolation can manifest itself into a hatred of or ambivalence towards society. Clearly this is the case with James. He feels he has been shunned, laughed at by his peers – all of them female. As a result he hates them.

'I used to imagine them being attacked,' he recalled. 'I would see their faces as they were being chased through the local park by a hooded man with a knife, who would catch them and rape them. It turned me on. I wanted to be that man. I wanted to hurt them. Get them back for what they'd done to me.'

Five years later, just before his 18th birthday, James readied himself to live out this sick fantasy. He stalked a girl, a complete stranger, then followed her home from a nearby school and willed himself to attack her. Thankfully for the girl, James didn't follow through on his plan. But he has hated teenage girls ever since. And his fantasies of revenge have grown to the point where they have been realised in his adult years – on much younger and more vulnerable victims.

'I wanted to make them suffer for what they did to me,' he said. 'I wanted to get them young before they could hurt another innocent like me.'

When you hear James talk about this development, it is hard to believe the words that are coming from his lips. He has the ability to disarm you with his honesty and, despite the chilling and repulsive subject matter of the conversation, his overwhelming charm. It therefore comes as no surprise to learn that his first victim was the seven-year-old daughter of his then girlfriend who he would regularly look after whenever his girlfriend was working.

James took on the role of father to the young girl, and showered her with love and affection. With his girlfriend, he'd take the youngster to the cinema, the park, and to the shopping malls to buy her presents. The threesome appeared for all intents and purposes to be the perfect family unit. The young girl even called him 'Daddy'.

'She [the girlfriend] never suspected a thing,' James revealed. 'She trusted me. Even when she found out about it, she refused to believe that it had happened. She couldn't believe that she had been blind to it, and didn't think I was capable of doing that.'

This boastful attitude is typical of the psychopath. James, it is clear, believes that he has gotten one over his ex-girlfriend. His glibness at having committed such a terrible act, and having gotten away with it for so long, is proof of his level of psychopathy. His immediate thoughts aren't with the victim or what his actions will have done to her psychologically, but are focused entirely upon himself and how clever he has been to have fooled someone who'd placed her trust in him, not to mention the safety and welfare of her child. It is as if he is almost bragging. As if he is saying, 'I can do whatever I want to do and I know I can get away with it'.

James sexually abused the young girl for a period of four years. During that time, he also assaulted two other girls – both of whom were sisters and happened to be the cousins of his first victim. He claims that he never had 'full sex' with any of the girls, the eldest of which was 14, although I seriously doubt this. 'I could never have done that. I didn't want to hurt them in that way. I just wanted to get rid of some of my anger and resentment at the time.'

James was eventually charged with offences under the Children and Young Persons Act and sentenced to three years in prison. During his jail term, he attended counselling sessions with sexual health therapists in a bid to change his behavioural make-up. While he acknowledges that he has a definite problem and that some of what he was taught in prison has helped him to recognise and understand the extent of his problem, James is unsure as to how effective those teachings will be.

'I know that what I did was wrong,' he said shaking his head and staring into space. 'I know that I should change, but whether I can is beyond my control.'

James is wrong. The ability to change is his and his alone. The truth of the matter is this: like many psychopaths James does not believe in change. He sees nothing wrong with his core being. He is a paedophile. A danger to every child he comes across or is allowed to spend time alone with. Yes, he can change. But he doesn't want to. Like many psychopaths currently living amongst us, he is happy the way he is.

***

While there are situational child molesters such as James all around us, the occurrence of the most horrifying and physically dangerous of preferential child molesters, the sadistic paedophile, is thankfully rare. These are the offenders who are rightly thought of (even amongst the criminal community) as being the lowest of the low. This is the type of evil individual who uses all of his psychopathic skills to gain complete control of his victims and then torture them for his own sexual gratification. Ian Brady and Myra Hindley were perhaps two of the best known sadistic paedophiles and the horror of their crimes, even though they were committed well over 30 years ago still live on to this day. Fred and Rosemary West are another killer couple who used children (including their own daughter) to sate their horrific sexual appetites.

Why does this happen? How can someone clinically abduct, torture, sexual abuse and then murder a child? Having read this far into Touched By The Devil, you, the reader, will know the answers to these questions. It happens because the offender is pathologically programmed to kill. He, or she, has been developing mentally and physically for many years, running it over and over in his mind, enjoying the erotic thrill his fantasies bring. They are ticking time-bombs, primed and ready to explode. Their minds are whirlwinds of sickeningly twisted and obscure thoughts. They don't see people as being humans, but rather mere vessels that they will lead, guide, dominate and control and finally, when the moment is perfect, snuff out. And who easier to control than the six-year-old schoolgirl they walk past every afternoon in the park, as she makes her way home? The pretty girl, all innocence and pigtails, walking home alone, totally unaware that she is being watched by the eyes of a wild human who is counting the seconds until he strikes. That is how it happens. We don't have to tell you about the devastation these offenders cause. The pain and suffering they bring to innocent lives. We don't have to walk in their shoes to sense the fear and dread they instil in their victims. But we can relate one case that has touched our hearts. That of a nine-year-old Australian, Ebony Simpson.

Wanton destruction

She was pretty a girl, always smiling, always happy with life. Ever popular with her friends and siblings, Ebony Simpson was the kind of child who could light up a room with her cheeky grin and natural good looks. The youngest of three children, she was the only daughter to her parents, Peter and Christine, and the apple of their eye.

It was the middle of the winter in the small town of Bega, a little over 400km south of Sydney on the New South Wales Sapphire Coast located in a verdant valley, and famous throughout the country for its major industry and employer – Bega Cheese. Ebony was on her way home from school. The date was Wednesday, August 19, 1992. It was just after four o'clock in the afternoon and this would be Ebony's last day alive.

Just like every other day she hopped off her school bus less than half a kilometre from her home on Arina Road and set off walking, swinging her backpack containing her school books, heading for home and some welcome relief from the weight of her things. As she walked, she would have noticed a light coloured Mazda saloon car sitting beside the kerb a hundred or so metres ahead of her. It would have been hard to miss, standing there as it was with its boot and bonnet open and a man beside it, seemingly trying to fix it, or at the very least work out what had caused it break down.

Ebony was an intelligent and streetwise child, but nothing bad ever happened in Bega, save for the odd stolen horse, and as aware as she was of the importance of not talking to strangers, she wouldn't have been overly concerned as she made her way towards the car. And anyway, home was now only a minute or so away, now. Safety was within reach. Ebony continued walking, picking up the pace slightly just in case, and in doing so, walked straight into a well-conceived and cunningly contrived trap.

The man standing beside the car on that day was 29-year-old Andrew Garforth. He had waited for this day for weeks. In fact he had long been planning what was about to happen. Previous to this day he'd spent considerable time cruising around schools in the area, looking for a suitable victim. Andrew Garforth wanted to snatch a child. Snatch a child and have sex with her. Andrew Garforth, it would transpire was a sadistic paedophile. The worst kind of human devil there is.

It's possible that Garforth had seen Ebony earlier in the week, walking the same route home from school along Arina Road. It's also possible, and very likely, that he would have checked the exact times she alighted from the bus and began her walk towards home. He would have known that at just after 4pm, all would be quiet on Arina Road, save for the soft footsteps of an innocent nine-year-old girl.

Ebony Simpson knew none of this, but she would soon discover that the man with the broken down car was a lot more than just that. As she neared the rear of the dirt-covered Mazda, Garforth, his sights fixed firmly on her, made his lethal move. Checking that there were no witnesses to see what he was about to do, he slammed the bonnet of the car shut and made a grab for the young girl. Ebony saw him coming at her too late, and tried to fight him off as his arms closed around her torso and lifted her off the floor. But it was a one-sided fight, despite Garforth's skinny, waif-like build, and within seconds Ebony Simpson had been bundled into the Mazda's boot. Garforth, heart thumping in his chest and excitement rising, had quickly slammed that shut too, before jumping into the driver's seat, starting the car's engine and pulling away from the abduction site with a squeal of rubber. In all it took less than 15 seconds from start to finish. Ebony Simpson was gone.

Garforth knew exactly where he would take Ebony. Like any other psychopathic offender his only concerns were the fulfilment of his sick fantasy and not getting caught. He knew he needed somewhere quiet and out of the way to which to take his victim. A place where her screams couldn't be heard. A place safe from prying eyes. That place was seven kilometres away at the site of a local dam, nestled in the middle of a small State forest. It was here, as darkness began to fall that Garforth subjected Ebony Simpson to an attack so barbaric and sickening in nature that when hardened murder detectives involved on the case heard about it in interviews with Garforth, they openly wept.

They arrived at the dam after a speedy drive from Arina Road and within seconds of the car coming to a skidding halt at the end of the dirt track that led to the site, Garforth had hauled a terrified and crying Ebony out of the boot and had dragged her a few metres away from the vehicle. He subdued the now fighting Ebony by punching her repeatedly and then pushed her to the ground and began tearing the school uniform off her body. She fought her attacker harder, panicking him for a moment that she might actually escape. But Garforth was well-prepared for this eventuality. In his pocket was a strand of hi-fi speaker wire that he'd brought with him in case he needed to secure and tie up his victim. He'd planned hard for this, he'd tell police later. He didn't want it to be messed up. Quickly, he turned Ebony onto her back, yanked her arms behind her and tied them together. Now, he was ready for the focal point of his plan.

Ebony was systematically raped by Garforth and all the while she cried for the man to stop and begged him to let her go back to her mother. Garforth, in a frenzy now, continued to rape and beat the nine-year-old beneath him, ignoring her cries and whimpers. When he'd finished Garforth stood up, and looked down at the battered girl beneath him. Despite the severity of the assault, Ebony, sobbing and pleading for her mother and her life, managed to drag herself up into a sitting position. Garforth realised he had a problem on his hands with this brave little girl. But he was prepared even for this. He knew that his crime would involve more than just rape. He knew from the outset, that if all of his repulsive fantasies were ever to come true, then his victim had to die – he had to experience the ultimate feelings of dominance and control – and leave no witnesses to point their fingers at him. And it was this aspect of Ebony Simpson's needless murder that tugged at the public's heartstrings for years to come.

Picking Ebony up by the scruff of the neck, Garforth marched her to his car. Here, he used another piece of flex to tie her legs together. Not content with this, he then scrambled around the site near where the rape and sexual assault had taken place and began to collect rocks from the dirt track. These he placed in Ebony's already heavy backpack. Strapping the backpack to the pleading girl's bag, he carried her to the dam's edge and threw Ebony Simpson face first into the water. Ebony never stood a chance. She drowned within four minutes of hitting the water, but not before fighting with all her might for her life and screaming for help, while trying desperately to make it to the bank of the dam and safety which was just metres away.

'She shouted for help as I threw her in,' Andrew Garforth said, describing the moment to police officers shortly after his arrest in chilling and emotionless detail. 'I walked away and ignored her. When I left her she was trying to get to the bank. I thought at the time that she'd either drown or make it to the bank. I drove away soon after.'

Proving the depth of his psychopathy, Garforth helped with the police search for Ebony Simpson's body the very next day, when it became clear to the people of Bega that one of their own daughters had been abducted. But if Garforth thought he was being clever and getting one over the police and other search party members, he was mistaken. Witnesses poured forward, all of them claiming to have seen a light coloured Mazda with dirty, exhaust smoke-stained windows cruising the streets of Bega in the days leading to Ebony's disappearance. School teachers also came forward to inform police that they too had seen the car prowling around the school gates, and a number of Ebony's friends also revealed that a similar car had been seen following school buses in the area, including the one which took Ebony towards her home.

A sharp-eyed policeman became the hero of the hour, just moments into the search, when he spotted Garforth's car. A quick check on the registration plate revealed the owner's identity and when Garforth returned to the vehicle after his bout with Ebony's search party, he was questioned by police about witnesses' allegations and promptly confessed to Ebony's murder. At 12.15am on Friday, August 21, he lead police to the spot where he had left Ebony. Her bloated body, with its hands and feet still tied tightly together and the backpack still in place, was found soon afterwards awash on the dam's bank. Her cause of death was listed as drowning.

'You can never forget a moment like that, for as long as you live,' Peter Simpson, Ebony's father told us. 'My daughter was slaughtered and there were so many questions as to why and so much anger. Even the simplest of things become something major. Friendships fall apart, relationships fall apart. It's so hard. And all the time you know that your child suffered terribly and that thought never leaves you. It has never left me.'

Peter and Christine Simpson were thrust into the media spotlight in the days and weeks after Ebony's brutal death. In the years that have followed the case, Peter Simpson has developed a love-hate relationship with the media and he has cannily used them to help change the very core of the New South Wales justice system.

'Both Christine and I knew that because of Ebony and her death we were in a good position to get the message heard that changes to the laws governing sentencing and murderers should be made,' Peter said. 'I remember after Garforth was sentenced to life in jail that the media were camped outside the courtroom wanting me to comment about him and the case. I didn't want to waste that opportunity.'

Peter Simpson told the gathered throng of reporters that Ebony Simpson had got the death sentence, the Simpson family got the life sentence and Garforth got bed and breakfast. His comments made headlines across Australia. Pretty soon, Peter Simpson's voice was heard all over the country once more in relation with other murder cases, and within a matter of months he had unwittingly become an unofficial spokesman for the families of murder victims – something he was never comfortable with.

'What I set out to do was to make sure that the death of my only daughter had not been in vain,' he said. 'It just seemed like

Ebony's murder was such a senseless, useless act and to think that nothing good could come out of it, I just couldn't come to terms with that.'

Something good did come out of this tragic event, however. Along with the parents of Anita Cobby (whose case is profiled in Chapter 9) the Simpsons helped form the Homicide Victims Support Group in Sydney, which has since been responsible for over 140 changes to legislation in the state.

It is courage like that shown by Peter and Christine Simpson, as well as the numerous other families of the victims of psychopaths who speak out and let the voices of their loved ones be heard even after death, which gives hope to us all that we can beat these monsters and make our society safe.

Peril in the Home

Earlier in this chapter we mentioned that each week between one and two children are killed by their parents or carers in the United Kingdom. This is a cold, hard fact and one that needs to be addressed, and which, thankfully is in part through a new anti-child abuse campaign being run by the NSPCC.

'The vast majority of children are loved and well cared for. But over the last 30 years, hundreds of children have been beaten, starved, burned, suffocated, poisoned, shaken, strangled or stabbed to death by their parents,' comments, Mary Marsh, the director of the NSPCC. 'The level of child abuse killings in this country are a national disgrace. In the few months we have heard how toddlers Ainlee Walker and Carla Nicole Bone were tortured and finally killed by their parents. There has rightly been a huge groundswell of concern since the terrible killings of Holly Wells, Jessica Chapman and Milly Dowler. The NSPCC shares that concern, yet people should realise that more children are killed at home by their parents.'

The charity has launched a major campaign calling on the Government to reduce the number of child deaths by reforming the child protection laws. The charity's FULL STOP campaign aims to have government reduce the number of children killed each year by their parents or carers (the figure currently stands at 80) by as much as half within the next 10 years.

'The protection of children is of vital importance to the future of our country,' says Paul Burstow, MP (Lib Dem, Sutton & Cheam). 'A child dies every week as a result of abuse and more than 300,000 children at risk of abuse or neglect are placed on the child protection register every year. It is time to put real safeguards in place and work towards preventing abuse and promoting children's rights.'

So acute is the problem of child abuse in the UK that the United Nations has itself expressed concern about the figures and has called for urgent action to be taken. The NSPCC also commissioned a Mori survey asking members of the public who they thought was most likely to be responsible for child killings. Only 11 percent of respondents opted for the parent, compared with 17 percent for strangers, while 70 percent said stopping child abuse killings was one of the most important issues for the government to take action on. This subject was seen as more pressing than committing British forces to the war against Iraq (15 percent), joining the euro (8 percent) and banning fox hunting (4 percent).

'The government must reform the child protection system to make it fit for the 21st century,' says Marsh. 'We must make sure that no child slips through the net.'

So what makes parents and carers resort to the sort of crime that most of us cannot even stand to read about? And why have all of these children been so forgotten by the media and the public alike?

Clinical psychologist and author, Oliver James, believes he has some answers. 'There's not enough honesty about parenting, or about how much parents wish their children were dead sometimes,' he says. 'We just about manage to cope, with every conceivable advantage. But if you're being driven bonkers by a small child and you've got a history of abuse in your own childhood, relationship problems, money problems, drug problems – then it's surprising that there aren't more children murdered.'

Low self-esteem, domestic violent, family breakdowns, alcoholism and drug misuse are frequently cited to be among the most common causes of child cruelty and neglect. Therefore, it is safe to say that dysfunction, both past and present, plays a large part in this type of crime – much as it does in the overall psychological development of the psychopathic offender.

But why the lack of publicity? 'Being out of sight of the public eye, children killed by abuse or neglect also tend to be out of mind,' says Phillip Noyes, the director of public policy at the NSPCC. The decline in media coverage of these deaths, he believes, is the chief reason.

'Research that we commissioned found that this decline is largely due to an increasing emphasis in the media on family values. These type of child deaths, unlike those committed by strangers, put these values in question – something the media is not keen to do,' Noyes says.

The media are not the only reason for the lack of noise being made on behalf of these forgotten dead. Shortcomings in the recording of child deaths in official statistics, difficulties in determining the cause of death and the lack of a standard and coordinated approach to child deaths are also to blame.

Supporters of the NSPCC's campaign hope that things will change once the shocking truth about the numbers of children killed by their parents is brought more and more into the public domain. A number of stars are supporting the campaign, including singer Natalie Imbruglia, who says: 'We tend to think a child is most at risk from a stranger. But every week one or two children are killed in the UK by their parents or carers. The statistics are appalling. This is something that shouldn't be happening and we can all help to turn it around by being vigilant. Child protection is everyone's business. We must not turn a blind eye to children at risk.'

• The NSPCC Child Protection Helpline can be contacted on 0808 800 5000 or via email at help@nspcc.org.uk.

CHAPTER 6

Looking For Love, Attention
and Fame – Stalkers

T hey may not generate the sensational press of their serial killing and raping cousins. Nor may the thought of their acts strike terror into the hearts of the population. Nevertheless stalkers are dangerous. They do destroy lives. They are psychopaths. And they are out there now.

Stalking wasn't taken too seriously around the world as a crime until the early 1990s. Before then the mass public and the media in general perceived stalkers as demented individuals who obsessed about and followed celebrities. Certainly, the majority of reported cases appeared to support this supposition.

Celebrity stalkers are always guaranteed big headlines in newspapers around the world. Celebrated cases include those of Jodie Foster and her stalker, John Hinckley Jr, who later went on to shoot the then US president Ronald Reagan. The name Mark Chapman will forever be linked with that of John Lennon, after The Beatles' frontman was gunned down outside his New York apartment in 1980. Chapman had stalked Lennon for days and was convinced that he was actually the real Lennon and the John Lennon he shot was an imposter. To this day he maintains this belief and his innocence.

Stars such as Madonna, Tom Cruise, David Letterman and Gwyneth Paltrow have all been victims of stalkers, and in some cases have come close to being killed by their so-called fans.

The 1997 case of Gianni Versace, murdered by spree killer Andrew Cunanan, illustrates the evil potency of the stalker in its entirety. Here was a man, psychopathic in the extreme, who, having already taken the lives of five other victims across the United States, drove to the Miami, South Beach, home of the multimillionaire designer. Once there he stalked Versace over a period of days and finally shot him in the head at point blank range. It was alleged that Cunanan had a seething rage towards Versace as a result of the Italian designer's rebuff of him at a party. Cunanan never forgave Versace for turning him down and made him pay the ultimate price. Much like Mark Chapman almost 20 years earlier, and Robert Bardo – who killed up and coming actress Rebecca Shaeffer in 1989 – he is perhaps the ultimate celebrity stalker-killer.

Tragic as these murders were, what is perhaps more tragic is that there are millions of people around the world who have been, and are being, targeted by stalkers almost every day. These people are not Hollywood film stars, nor are they famous singers or designers. They are ordinary everyday people whose lives are turned upside down by the obsessive and sometimes lethal behaviour of stalkers.

A full statistical picture of stalking in the UK was published in October 2000 based on the British Crime Survey. It shows that about 4 per cent of women had been stalked in a 12 month period. However, 16.8 per cent of women between the ages of 16 and 19 had been stalked over those 12 months, a figure that the report described as 'worryingly high'. The total number of victims over the period covered was estimated to be a staggering 610,000 women, compared to 270,000 men. In around two thirds of all cases of stalking, regardless of what sex the victim is, there is the fear of violence.

The advent of the Internet has brought with it a new form of stalking – cyberstalking. This crime has been given huge exposure in the media and some researchers believe that instances of it are now more common than those of traditional stalking. While there are no hard figures to back this belief, while working on this book we discovered that cyberstalking is indeed very common, particularly amongst Internet chat room users. There are currently three primary ways in which cyberstalking is conducted: email stalking, Internet stalking and computer stalking.

Email stalking is by far the most common form with victims often on the receiving end of hate, obscene and threatening email. Email cyberstalkers are not content with simply frightening their targets and have also been known to send their victims viruses and high volumes of junk mail that clog up their systems.

'In many ways stalking via email represents the closest replication of traditional stalking patterns,' Dr Emma Ogilvie, a pioneering criminology expert in the subject told us. 'As with stalking in the real world, it can result from an attempt to initiate a relationship, or desire to threaten and traumatise a person.'

Internet stalking is a far more public form of email stalking and in almost all cases involves a victim who is a frequent user of Internet chat rooms. Worryingly, this type of stalking can, and often does, spill over into the real world.

'In these instances, cyberstalking is accompanied by traditional stalking methods such as threatening phone calls, vandalism of property, threatening mail and physical attacks,' says Dr Ogilvie.

Computer stalking is a whole lot more complicated and requires a more sophisticated stalker for this to occur. Relatively few cases of computer stalking – whereby the stalker takes control of a person's computer via the Internet – have been recorded. However, despite the, up until now, rare instances of this type of criminal activity, it is still considered a serious threat to individual rights and freedom.

While email and Internet stalking can be beaten by adopting defensive techniques (such as turning off the computer, changing contact details such as an email address, ending participation in a chat room, etc), computer stalkers exploit the inner workings of the Internet and the global Windows operating system, to assume control of the computer of their targeted victim. It may sound far-fetched and impossible, but it is happening.

'It is probably not widely recognised that an individual computer connected to the Internet can be identified, and connected to another computer via the Internet,' says Ogilvie, who has spent the past year researching all aspects of stalking and cyberstalking. 'This connection is not the link via a third party that characterises typical Internet interactions. Rather it is a computer-to-computer connection allowing the stalker to exercise control over the computer of the target.'

While a high level of knowledge of computers and the inner workings of the Internet are needed for this kind of stalking to take place, Ogilvie warns that inevitably, 'more cases are going to come to light as instructions on how to use the technologies in this way become available on the Internet'.

Whether a traditional or virtual stalker, it is important to distinguish between the different types of offender that there are, and in so doing, clear up any discrepancies there might be regarding stalkers' behaviour and psychological characteristics.

In the 1998 British Crime Survey, which featured a lengthy discourse on stalkers, the authors of the report classified stalkers as occurring in four distinctive groups, based on a victim/offender relationship and the sex of the victim. These groups are:

- Female victim – intimate relationship with the offender.
- Female victim – non-intimate relationship with the offender.
- Male victim – intimate relationship with the offender.
- Male victim – non-intimate relationship with the offender.

An intimate relationship is one where the offender is known to the victim through an emotional attachment and includes spouses or former spouses, relatives, close friends and former romantic partners. A non-intimate stalker is classed as a stranger, casual acquaintance, manager/colleague at work, or a member of the public contacted through work.

While this is one descriptive way of describing the typology of stalkers based upon the characteristics of their victims, it doesn't give a true psychological evaluation of who they are and why they do what they do. Therefore we will use three terms to classify stalkers that are employed by the majority of law enforcement agencies and psychologists around the world. These terms – the simple obsessional, the love obsessional and the erotomanic stalker – best describe the mental and psychological characteristics of this type of individual.

Each of these stalker types is very different in terms of how they think and behave, as each one has a very different motivation underlying their stalking behaviour.

Erotomania, also referred to as de Clerambault's Syndrome, has a lengthy history of coverage in psychiatric literature. The term refers to a delusional belief that one is passionately loved by another individual, usually someone of higher social status. This could include media personalities, superiors at work or acquaintances in social circles. The erotomanic – as people suffering from this symptom are called – typically tends to engage in excessive efforts to contact the person they are obsessed with.

Erotomanic stalkers are commonly female, whereas the other two types of stalker are more commonly males. However, male erotomanics do occur and they act out their fantasy with greater force than their female counterparts, and are often more deadly. Andrew Cunanan (see page 126) and Robert Bardo are good examples of this. The erotomanic stalker is motivated by a relationship that is based upon the stalker's psychological fixation. This fantasy is commonly expressed in such forms as 'fusion', where the stalker blends his or her personality into the target's, or 'erotomania', where a fantasy is based upon idealised romantic love or the spiritual union of the stalker and the victim rather than sexual union.

Motivation can also come via religious fantasies or voices directing the offender to a targeted individual. This preoccupation with the target becomes all-consuming and ultimately can lead to the target's death.

The fusion of reality and fantasy results in the erotomanic stalker genuinely believing that the victim is a part of them. This pushes them to contact the victim repeatedly in an effort to realise their desire for a fusion of identity. In extreme circumstances, the stalker can believe that the only way a victim will be at one with them is through their combined mutual death, or for the stalker to be noticed by their victim as a result of such acts as the assassination of a powerful or celebrated person.

The offender has little to no insight into the fact that in reality there is no relationship between themselves and the victim. Communication can be achieved through both delusional means, such as a media personality sending 'personal subliminal messages' to the stalker via the TV, to non-delusional means such as letters and gifts being sent directly to the chosen target.

When it comes to the length of time devoted to stalking, the erotomanic is in it long term. The stalking activity is the sole focus of their life. Letters and telephone calls, surveillance of their target's daily activities, together with repeated attempts to approach them personally are all part of the erotomanic's repertoire. With the passage of time, and a general increase in the stalker's frustration, the activity increases in intensity, potentially becoming all-consuming, leading to the death or injury of either the victim or someone else.

The majority of erotomanic attacks are close range and confrontational. These attacks are usually spontaneous, as reflected in the stalker's more haphazard approach to the target. Evidence is usually left behind and there are likely to be witnesses. The stalker still plans and fantasises about the stalking, but takes advantage of any opportunity to contact the target.

The erotomanic almost always has his or her target under constant surveillance. There are repeated attempts to contact the target via mail or telephone calls, gifts and visits to their home or place of employment. It's not unusual for the police to take action to remove the stalker from one or both of these locations, following an initial complaint from the victim.

So what will this type of stalker sound like if he or she manages to talk to you? For a start, the conversation will reflect the preoccupation with the fantasy relationship or life with the victim. Those associated with the stalker will recall their total focus on this relationship in their conversations. The stalker may claim to have a relationship with the victim, fabricating stories – both in his own mind and to people he knows – to support this belief system. His stories will usually be very convincing and allay any suspicions.

Similar to the erotomanic, the love obsessional stalker is also characterised by the absence of any prior relationship between the victim and the stalker. Quite often here, as in erotomanic cases, the victim is known through the media, though there are also a number of instances in which the victim is simply an ordinary person who falls prey to this type of stalker.

In contrast to the erotomanic, a large number of love obsessional stalkers suffer from schizophrenia or bipolar affective disorder – a mental disorder marked by periods of excitation and depression. Many are socially maladjusted and have seldom, if ever, been involved in a meaningful intimate relationship.

This type of stalker usually believes that they are a fantastic person who could give the victim an incredibly meaningful relationship, becoming their ideal lover. The only problem with this belief, however, is that the victim does not know them, and may not particularly want to. However, this is not a problem as far as this type of stalker is concerned. They believe that once the victim does get to know them, they will see what a beautiful person they are and fall in love with them. This belief is completely unrealistic. However, the stalker's mission at this early stage is to allow the victim to get to know him, hence the repeated letters and telephone calls in which he expresses his adoration of her and his desire to meet her. The intensity of the content contained in these letters is often very disturbing to the victim, and is usually the first indication that there is a severe problem.

As time elapses and the stalker receives no response he becomes increasingly frustrated and angry, and may physically confront the victim. This period of anger and frustration may last for a long time, as the self-esteem and identity of the stalker are inextricably intertwined with his success at wooing the victim, effectively proving to himself that he is the perfect soul mate. He believes that all he has to do to win the affections of his victim is to show his depth of love for her to the rest of the world.

Entering the mind of a love obsessional stalker allows us to understand why these feelings surface. Imagine for a moment that you are a person who has never experienced a meaningful relationship with anybody else. You like to think that you are a sincere, loving person who simply has not had the opportunity to 'give yourself' completely to another person. Deep down you have a low sense of self-esteem, as you realise that no one has ever loved you as you think you deserve to be loved.

As a child, you were not shown that you were loved unconditionally, or perhaps you were never shown love at all. Whatever happened, you do not feel confident enough to directly approach a woman and ask her out on a date. You feel unable to accept a negative answer and believe that the reason she might say no to you is because you are not a good enough person for her to be seen with, and therefore she does not believe that you could be her soul mate.

Perhaps this girl is someone who serves you at the supermarket each week, and she once showed you some affection by asking if you would like help with packaging your shopping. Nobody has ever cared about you enough to ask you this before, so you begin to believe that perhaps she is the right person for you. She is your one true love.

You decide to follow her home. You manage to get her address and perhaps her phone number through some illicit means. You send her flowers every day, because you believe in your mind that this is what people do to show affection. You write her long, intense, and often passionate letters expressing your love and desire for her. You tell her repeatedly how much you adore her.

You get no response. She obviously doesn't understand the extent of your feelings. Maybe she is avoiding you because she is married, or put off by the intensity of your actions. Maybe she doesn't even know you, and hasn't seen you in the flesh. Whatever the reason, she ignores you. She rejects you completely, shattering your sense of self-worth in the process. Your mind tells you that the reason she has ignored you is because she doesn't know who you are. You decide that you will do something about this and make her know you, make her understand your feelings for her.

You start by sending her more flowers and chocolates. You bombard her with more letters, pouring your heart out with every sentence, telling her how much you want her, need her, love and respect her – all the things you believe she wants to hear. Eventually, your persistence pays off. She contacts you. Not to say how happy she is to hear from you, however, but to tell you to leave her alone.

It doesn't matter to you that she has told you to stop. In your mind, life is beautiful – she is speaking to you. You now have a relationship. You may be quarrelling, as most couples do, and she may not be saying what you want to hear, but she is speaking to you. All you need to do now is make her admit to herself that she does indeed want and need a relationship with you. This may happen by intensifying the relationship – in other words, increasing the stalking behaviour.

After some time of trying desperately to have a relationship with this woman and being rejected – having her say through her actions that you are no good – you become rather annoyed and frustrated with the whole situation. However, you have invested too much of yourself in the relationship to date, and you know that you are this person's soul mate. You are in love with this person, you can feel it surging through your system and you know that love requires persistence and effort. You will prove that you love her by continuing in the face of adversity.

At the same time you start to hate this person who is rejecting you. These ambivalent feelings are unpleasant. At times you are so angry that you want to hurt or maybe even kill her. At other times your love for her knows no bounds and you will do anything to prove this and have her accept you.

Imagine this cycle continuing over and over again. Imagine the frustration, the anger, the hurt and damage to your self-esteem. The pain and humiliation, the belief that nobody wants or loves you, when you try and demonstrate your love for someone – albeit in an inappropriate way because you have never known how to express love, or even what love is.

Imagine wanting to love someone so desperately that you will do anything to have them, yet at the same time being someone who does not even understand the true concept of love because it is something you have never experienced. This is the world of the love-obsessional stalker.

Finally we have the simple obsessional stalker. This type of stalking usually happens when the victim and the stalker have some prior knowledge of one another. They are the most common cases, and also the most dangerous.

Although the minority of simple obsessional stalking cases do not involve an intimate relationship, a significant number of cases are a result of these intimate relationships gone sour – for example, ex-husband/wife or ex-dating partners.

Many of these cases are the result of a domestic violence situation in which one of the partners (the abused) finds the courage to break away from the relationship, only to discover their partner is intent on a campaign of harassment, intimidation and mental terror. The stalker's motives may be to coerce the victim back into the relationship or simply to seek revenge by making the victim's life as miserable as possible. Quite often they succeed in the latter.

In contrast to the domestic violence situation, many relationships involve nothing more than brief dating, with one of the partners deciding not to continue the contact. Such break-ups are simply a part of everyday life where two people (or one of the two) realise they are not compatible. In certain situations, however, the rejected partner may have an unrealistically high degree of emotional investment in the relationship. He – and these stalkers are typically male – may become angry at the loss of control and what he feels is an attack on his self-image. He may also become frustrated by what he perceives as his mistreatment, or the feeling that he has been 'led on' by his former partner. This can lead to physical threats and actual harm in an attempt to gain revenge and show the victim exactly who is in control – in this case, the stalker. What the stalker fails to realise is that in terrorising another person he will never be in control of himself.

The other major category of simple obsessional cases involves non-intimate situations that often occur in the work environment. One such situation involves the suspended or terminated employee who perceives that a particular supervisor is the primary cause of his or her troubles. A pattern of stalking behaviour develops aimed at terrorising this innocent victim. We have come across cases throughout the corporate world that have led to direct confrontation, and even violence, because intervention was not sought early enough.

Another common case within the workplace involves the employee, usually male, who attempts to establish a personal relationship with a co-worker and has his advances rejected. Similar to the dating situation, these individuals continue to impose themselves on the victim to the point where, having been unsuccessful, their adoration rapidly turns to anger and a pattern of stalking begins.

A variety of other non-intimate relationships exist within the simple obsessional type. The largest group involves people who have had some form of prior professional relationship, such as doctor/patient, psychologist/client, teacher/student or one-time business partners. Others include neighbours, schoolmates, flatmates and friends. As with the workplace violence cases, the stalker may be seeking either an intimate relationship with the victim or wanting vengeance for some real or imagined act of mistreatment.

Letters and flowers are not weapons of choice for the simple obsessional stalker. For them, psychological intimidation and physical force are keys to overpowering their victims. They destroy them physically and mentally until the victims begin to feel that the stalker is their only hope. By reducing the victim to his own insecure level, the stalker makes the victim believe that they are worthless and that out of all the people on earth, the stalker is the only person who will accept them and love them. In destroying them, the psychopath eases the psychological burden on himself by seeing the victim as someone who is beneath him.

From this viewpoint we can see where all of the physical and psychological acts of terror and possessiveness arise with the simple obsessional stalker. Quite clearly these individuals – and there are many of them out there today – have a deep-seated insecurity with themselves and with their status in life.

They may have positions of power, or be the lowliest of workers. But their feelings of insecurity remain the same, whatever their social and professional standing. It is this insecurity which leads to their dangerousness if their identity, sense of self-worth and status in the world are challenged, or even shattered by their victim's rejection of them.

No matter which stalker you might come across and what actions they take, one constant remains – these individuals are all dangerous and equally destructive. While a serial killer may use a knife or a hammer to terrify his victim into submission, and the rapist may use a balaclava, rope and kind words to get what he wants, the stalker will use seemingly innocuous objects such as flowers, chocolates, perfume and passionately written letters and emails.

Whatever weapons they choose, psychopaths are psychopaths – it doesn't matter what they do or how they do it. They are dangerous. They are self-serving. They are emotionless. And some of the worse psychopaths there are, and maybe even the most lethal when one considers their full potential and bizarre state of mind, are stalkers.

Katie

Katie had never met Jeff. She had no idea who he was, what he looked like, or where he came from. He came out of nowhere and turned her world upside down within the space of a year. Every night since that first day he came into her life, Katie has asked herself over and over again why it all happened and what she did that was so wrong that made her the target of a particularly brutal stalker.

Likewise, Jeff had never met Katie. He too had no idea what she looked like and knew nothing about her life until the point where he came into it. None of this mattered to him. Divine intervention had brought them together. An act of God in the shape of a business card innocently placed in a glass jar on top of a trendy bar by Katie, in the hope that it would be picked out and win her an all expenses paid weekend break at a top hotel.

For the next year a relationship would develop between the two during which Jeff would beseech Katie for a chance for them both to meet and prove in person the love he had for her.

'When he first emailed me and told me how he thought I was attractive and was someone he admired, I was very flattered and not a little surprised,' Katie told us. 'He said we'd met briefly at a business conference. I meet so many people in my job that I honestly couldn't remember whether I'd met him or not. I'm pretty careful who I give my contact details to anyway, so I thought it might have been true.'

Of course it wasn't the truth. Jeff had seen Katie's business card pressed against the glass jar. According to what he later told Katie when his stalking reached a peak, he liked the design of the company logo, fished out the card, and read Katie's name. He decided to keep it, he said, 'because it made me feel warm' and he thought 'Katie was a name he could love for the rest of his life'.

Analysing the early aspects of this case, it is clear to see that this individual genuinely believed a normal relationship could evolve – if only Katie took the time to get to know him. This is a typical case of a love obsessional stalker. Jeff believes that Katie is the most beautiful and fantastic person in the world. He knows this because he feels they are soul mates. He does not even need to talk to her to realise she is such a special person. The fact they have not met further confirms for him that she is the right one – he knows she is amazing simply by thinking about her.

Jeff believes that his feelings and actions are completely normal, because this is how he interprets love. He has seen in the media that people fall in love at first sight and live happily ever after, and this confirms his feelings in this situation. He feels it must be normal because he has seen it so many times on TV and read about it in books and magazines. He also believes that love is hard work and that relationships are difficult, so he must try and be persistent to win the heart of Katie. He must therefore swamp her with gifts of flowers and declarations of his love. He feels like he is exposing himself to her in demonstrating his love, and in doing this Katie will realise what a fantastic person he is and fall madly in love with him.

That first email was the beginning of a deluge of such

protestations of supposed love and affection from Jeff to Katie. An hour after she read the message, another appeared in her inbox. This one was less subtle and more sinister in what it said, and made Katie realise very early on that Jeff was someone she didn't particularly want to be around:

'I am surprised and sad that you have not responded to me yet,' it read. 'You must be very busy, or maybe just plain rude … You should make some time for yourself. Have some fun. How about a movie, some dinner, a few drinks, with me, one night this week? Give me a call when you can, please. I won't take no for an answer, so make sure you say yes. Thinking of you constantly. I can't get you out of my mind.'

Two hours later, three dozen red roses arrived at her desk. 'I knew they were from him immediately,' Katie said. 'The girls in the office were laughing and joking about it and saying how romantic it was, but when I saw the flowers I felt sick. It was like my personal space was being invaded.'

On the surface the behaviour of this individual does not appear threatening. How can sending roses and gifts as tokens of love possibly be threatening behaviour? It is the underlying significance or psychology behind these acts that makes them sinister. His actions are a deliberate invasion of Katie's privacy and gives the offender a feeling of power and control over her. This ensures he is constantly on her mind and in her thoughts, which is exactly where he wants to be.

Essentially this type of stalker wants to be only the thing that the victim thinks about. They want to be the entire world for the victim. It is this that is represented by the flowers, not some form of love. In fact, the stalker often does not even realise what true love is, as they have never experienced it themselves. For some, love is equivalent to owning somebody, to having the possessive relationship they see depicted in the media and feel that they are entitled to.

This man has absolutely no insight into the delusional nature of his beliefs – predominantly because he has no true insight into what either a relationship, or love, actually is. He believes that his obsessive behaviour and the act of picturing his victim in his head and feeling like she is the one for him, is a relationship. If you talked to this man and questioned his actions and beliefs, you would come away with the opinion that he had no idea whatsoever what a real relationship was or how to go about starting one. At this point in the case, he would also say that he does in fact have a relationship with Katie. In addition, the people close to him in life would believe that he was involved intimately with Katie from the way he would talk about her.

That night Katie pondered what to do. The next day, she arrived at work, determined to put Jeff in his place and get him to leave her alone for good. Before she could do so, however, a new message was waiting to be read.

'You are very ungrateful aren't you? I tell you how I feel, show you my affection and I get nothing in return. How could you do this to someone? I wouldn't treat an animal like you are treating me. You should be more open, Katie. You should give me a chance. Come on, call me. Have some fun. I'm waiting and longing to hear you say my name. Love, Jeff.'

Having read Jeff's latest words, Katie made what was to prove a bad choice. She picked up the telephone and dialled the number Jeff had included with his messages. She told him in no uncertain terms that she didn't much care for what he was doing and that while she was flattered by the attention she had no desire to take it any further.

'I basically told him to leave me alone and get a life,' Katie said. 'I was pretty short with him and didn't let him respond to me. It was like I was talking to a bad child. I felt terrible afterwards and did feel sorry for him. He sounded crushed. I never expected to hear from him again.'

Far from being crushed, Jeff would have been thrilled by Katie responding to his letter and explaining the pain he was causing her. As far as he's concerned there is now communication between himself and his love object. He is still able to demonstrate his love for her through speaking with her. Katie feeling sorry for him would be interpreted as her showing him that she does have feelings and does care for him.

This is precisely what happened. Rather than putting Jeff off, Katie's emotional response encouraged his belief that what he felt for her was indeed right and that she felt the same way. Katie's call enabled Jeff to feel good about the developing 'relationship'. Very quickly, he escalated his level of correspondence with her and managed to get email messages through to Katie despite her changing her address on an almost weekly basis.

'It became a trial for me to do my job,' Katie says. 'Emails, faxes, letters, flowers, perfume, chocolates. That's what my days were filled with. I was angry and annoyed and told him so whenever he called me. It seemed to spur him on. Looking back, I should have kept my emotions in check and ignored him, but it's hard to do that when someone is in your face constantly and you don't have any idea why.'

A transfer interstate brought Katie new hope that she would be rid of Jeff's attentions once and for all. Of course she wasn't.

'He found out where I'd been transferred to and continued to hound me,' she revealed. 'The letters and the messages kept coming. This man was driving me insane. I felt like I was being emotionally and mentally raped. There was nothing I could do to escape his attention.'

One other mistake Katie made was not going to the police early on to report Jeff's stalking.

'At the time, I thought that it [me going to the police] would only antagonise him more,' she said. 'I thought, wrongly now I know, that I could handle him by myself. Looking back I should have gone to the police the first moment this guy came into my life. Maybe then it wouldn't have lasted for so long.'

After two years of having him constantly in her life, at the time of writing, Katie has heard nothing from Jeff for 10 months. We suspect the reason for this is because Jeff is either dead (often the only way a stalker will actually stop hounding his victim) or, more likely, has been sentenced to a prison term for some other offence. Equally likely is the fact that he might have found someone else to stalk.

We can't say whether this is the case however, because like

Katie, we don't know who Jeff is exactly and despite some thorough investigative work on our part could not trace him or his present location. All that is left behind of him are a few messages that Katie saved and the mental scars that will be with her forever.

For now, Katie is trying to lead as normal a life as possible. Thoughts of Jeff are always on her mind and she often catches herself looking over her shoulder as she walks down a street, convinced that she is being watched and followed by a dark presence that wishes her ill.

'My life will never be the same again, no matter where I am or what I do,' she told us. 'I'm trying to put the pieces of my life back together and regain some of the sparkle that he took away. I'm trying hard, but it is difficult. I hope he is dead. I hope he never returns.'

CHAPTER 7

Peril in the Workplace

T he common perception of a psychopath is that of the stalking, bloodthirsty killer who commits the most sickening and depraved of acts on terrified, often female, victims.

The truth of the matter is somewhat different, however. While many psychopaths are indeed serial killers and rapists, these types of individuals are far less common than the psychopath who doesn't need to derive pleasure and sexual gratification from killing.

The psychopath who derives a feeling of power and control resulting from the psychological – rather than the physical – destruction of other people is far more common. It is estimated that for every serial killer and other more extreme form of psychopath, there are 20,000 others out there in society, living and working alongside you, who attain feelings of power and control through means other than physical destruction. This equates to approximately 3 to 5 per cent of the adult male population, and 0.5 to 1 per cent of the adult female population.

Psychological destruction can be incredibly devastating. We have come across individuals suffering from nervous breakdowns, depression, guilt, physical devastation and a whole range of symptoms. It is definitely not uncommon to witness these symptoms resulting from a psychopathic boss, spouse or relative. Consultative work undertaken by us on behalf of major organisations and individuals aimed at uncovering what are commonly termed white-collar psychopaths, has revealed that the instances of such psychopathy are increasing. It is clear from our work and research for *Psychopaths,* that white-collar psychopathy is a major legal and social issue that is more common than many of us are led to believe.

It is perhaps a mistake however to label these types of offenders as simply white-collar psychopaths. While this term has been used correctly by many psychologists and experts to describe psychopaths who work as doctors, lawyers, bankers, accountants, brokers and so on, there are just as many of this type of offender working in the blue collar world. You don't have to be paid a fortune and wear a suit to be terrifying. Even the garage mechanic can be menacing and conniving.

The psychological processes employed by these types of psychopath are fundamentally the same as those employed by serial killers and rapists. Each craves the feelings of total power and control over their own lives through attempting to dominate other people, or by being ruthless towards others.

Just as the serial killer derives a sense of power and control from the murder and torture of a person, the white-collar psychopath derives the same feelings from the destruction of an individual's self-esteem at work. This can be done through the instigation of often barbaric initiation ceremonies at a club or workplace, the defrauding of millions of dollars from a company, or from the simple belief that no one else in the world is as intelligent as they are.

A number of general behavioural and psychological characteristics can be used to identify these individuals within society, though they should be used with extreme caution and even then only by professionals. In addition, some but not all of the characteristics presented here may be possessed by many people you know and possibly love. What is important is the number of these traits the person has and their relative importance and value in that person's lifestyle.

In general, psychopaths are glib and superficial, egocentric and grandiose, show a lack of remorse or guilt, exhibit a lack of empathy, are deceitful and manipulative, and possess shallow emotions. Their lifestyle is often characterised by impulsive behaviour, poor behavioural controls, a need for excitement, a lack of responsibility, early behaviour problems and antisocial behaviour.

White-collar psychopaths possess a high number of these character traits. They are often individuals who, by their very profession and position within it, we are supposed to trust implicitly, but they shatter that trust with their cold-bloodedness and deceit. As we will show, power, position and influence can be used just as lethally as a hammer, knife or piece of rope.

Helenna

It was Helenna's dream job. The chance to start again after a painful divorce. The chance for her to finally focus solely on her career and not concentrate all of her physical and mental energy on an overbearing partner. The perfect chance for her to steer her life back onto the path she wanted.

The marriage had been floundering like a ship lost at sea in the midst of a storm for five years. Three children, all conceived in rapid succession, had prevented Helenna from contemplating a serious career. This bubbly and striking woman was unable to even begin to think about a vocation in the way she wanted, let alone plan one.

'We were growing apart, I had sacrificed so much to be a dutiful wife and mother and I felt I was suffering mentally for it,' Helenna said. 'My husband worked hard and was hardly ever home. He was a good father in limited ways, but I knew that somewhere, some place, there had to be something better.'

The chance to find out came as the couple were meeting with solicitors to discuss the terms of their divorce.

Before her marriage, Helenna had worked as a juvenile care worker, protecting the rights of vulnerable children and young adults. Flicking through the newspaper one Saturday morning, she saw a job advertised for a child welfare officer in a different town. Helenna saw the position as an escape hatch and a chance for her to throw off the shackles of her past.

'I applied for the job and dreamt about it every night,' she revealed. 'I wanted it so badly, I almost burst into tears when, two weeks later, the supervisor of the unit called on the telephone, interviewed me, and offered me the job. I accepted on the spot. I was so thrilled. I couldn't believe it. Finally something good was happening to me. Something all of my own doing. I was very proud of myself.'

Helenna promised her new boss that she would leave for her new home a week later. For now, the children would stay with their father until she found a new place to live, and had settled into her new surrounds. Then they would move to be with her, in accordance with the custody arrangement agreed as part of the divorce.

The day before she left a former colleague called her out of the blue. 'He said that he'd heard about my new job and that he felt he should warn me about my new boss,' revealed Helenna. 'He said he [the new boss] had a problem with women, and was a "complete bastard".'

Helenna listened and dismissed her friend's words. 'After all, I'd been through and survived a pretty tough divorce, and thought I could handle anything,' she said. Within a week of arriving, Helenna had found a house to live in and had been given a full tour of the area where she would work. She found her new boss to be charming, not at all like she'd been expecting.

'He was helpful and came across as very caring and dedicated to his work,' Helenna said. 'This was a relief because there would only be the two of us in the unit and if we were to have any success we would have to work and get along well together.'

After her first week's familiarisation, the work began to quickly pile up on Helenna's new desk. Counselling sessions crammed her diary, clients called in regularly and she found that she was working straight 14-hour days.

'I didn't mind this,' she said. 'It was all still exciting, being independent again.' What her excitement prevented her from seeing, however, were the first indications of her new boss's unusual behaviour.

'I remember thinking at the time that there was a lot of work and that he didn't seem to do much,' she said. 'In fact, because I was so busy I simply accepted his absences from the office as part and parcel of the department's workings. He would rush into the office at odd times of the day, and rush back out again saying that he had another urgent appointment. He was very charming about it, said that he'd help me out later when he returned and so on. Of course, he never did.'

Helenna later found out that her manager's so-called 'urgent appointments' were in fact illicit meetings and sex sessions with his three mistresses who he would visit at various times of the day, every day.

With the work continuing to pile up, Helenna was dealt a shattering blow in her second month at the job. Her children came to visit her for a Bank Holiday weekend. After a couple of days frolicking on the beach and enjoying the summer sun, Helenna's eldest son, James, took her aside and told her that the three of them would not be moving to her new home.

'I didn't know what to say. I was devastated. The four of us spent the whole of Sunday crying. It was the saddest day of my life. They left the next day, all of us still crying and I suddenly felt very much alone and extremely vulnerable.'

Her manager noticed this vulnerability. His reaction to it and to Helenna's sadness over the episode with her children is a classic example of the complete lack of empathy white-collar psychopaths display for those around them.

Firstly, he bombarded Helenna with work. He refused to talk to her about cases they were supposed to work on together, telling her that he had more important things to think about and that if she couldn't handle it then she could leave.

Helenna struggled under the increasing weight of the workload, and was often forced to work up to 18 hours a day simply to keep up. She hardly slept at night, worrying about what the next day would bring, wondering how she would cope. All the while, the feelings of loneliness and vulnerability increased, leaving her an emotional and physical wreck.

'This went on for about eight months,' she told us, still visibly shaken by her ordeal. 'I looked a mess, felt shocking inside and was picked on and criticised constantly by him. All the charm that he had showered me with when I first arrived had vanished within a few months. I began to see him for what he was. A vile, lying, conniving bully who was making my life a total misery.'

In Helenna's story we can see the psychopathic characteristics manifesting themselves in a number of very important ways. Essentially a lack of consideration or feeling for any other human being apart from himself is the most important factor observed so far in Helenna's boss. He displays absolutely no conscience or regard for Helenna, seeing the world as being one where only the fittest and most cunning survive. He would genuinely believe that there was absolutely nothing wrong with any of the behaviours described.

From his perspective, life is functioning perfectly. He has a person to do all of his work for him and she satisfies his deep-seated need to feel in control over someone who is weaker and more vulnerable than he is. This is clearly shown by his bullying of Helenna. Her reactions to him would actually please and encourage him to continue with his behaviour. He is able to have sexual intercourse with numerous people, satisfying his high sexual drive and also his need for constant excitement and stimulation. It is highly likely he also got a thrill from the 'illicit' nature of the affairs and the fact that he could be caught by his employers, colleagues and his wife. This 'challenge' would have heightened the pleasure of the experience.

His glibness, superficial nature and charm allow him to also take credit for Helenna's work. He is being positively reinforced for every single one of his devastating behaviours. Both the pleasure he experiences from the actual power and control in the acts themselves, and the fact that he is being paid to be cruel to people, feeds his psychopathy. The added fact that he is being rewarded professionally by his bosses for being so productive adds to the thrill and further justifies his callous actions in his mind.

Helenna would spend what time she had at the weekends crying. Depressed and lonely, she would telephone her children and talk to them for hours on end. She would cross off the days on her calendar, longing for the school holidays when her children would come and visit her. Her work prevented her from meeting anyone other than her clients and patients. Her boss prevented her from taking a break, constantly pushing her on, forcing her to take on new projects and develop new services, for which he would inevitably take the credit.

'My life was hell,' Helenna said. 'In the end, I said to myself enough! I couldn't cope with the constant barrage of abuse from him, the seemingly endless lies, and the lack of appreciation. I went for help.'

Helenna decided to take the step of reporting her boss to the regional manager for the area. Her words fell on deaf ears and left her incredulous.

'I sat there for three hours in the regional manager's office and let it all out,' Helenna remembered. 'I told him everything, the affairs, the misuse of funds and equipment, the lack of supervision and interest, the abuse, the whole works. The guy laughed at me, said my manager was one of the finest counsellors and care workers in the state, and told me I was the one with the problem and that I should be the one getting help. I couldn't help but cry. I felt betrayed by what I was hearing. I left completely bewildered and in shock.'

Worse was to come. By the time she'd arrived back home, her manager had heard all about her trip to Cairns. At 10.30 on a Friday night he knocked on Helenna's front door.

'He said he needed to talk to me, that there were some things I needed to understand, that I needed to learn,' Helenna revealed, her voice shaking with emotion as she recalled the scene. 'His eyes terrified me, his whole demeanour was aggressive. I was scared to death. There was no way on earth that I was letting him into the house.'

Helenna's manager threatened her verbally saying that if she ever went behind his back again, he would make her pay. He also said that she was weak and pathetic and that she was worthless. He claimed that the only reason she got the job in the first place was because nobody else would take it. If he had his time over, he said to her, he would never have bothered to phone her in the first place and offer her the job.

This irrational logic comes from the manager's instability and insecurity. His aim is to inflict as much emotional pain as possible on his targeted victim. This is the typical aggressive behaviour often exhibited by a white-collar psychopath.

Helenna described her terror to us as tears ran down her face, the memories of that night all too clear in her head despite the passage of time.

'I told him to go. He refused. Just stood there, staring at me. I slammed the door shut and locked it. He began to kick it, screaming at me to let him in. I slumped behind the door shaking with fear, crying and gasping for breath. It went on for 40 minutes. Forty terrifying minutes during which I thought I was going to die at his hands.'

Every now and again, the banging and screaming would stop and silence would return. Helenna would crawl to her living room to look through the window to see if her manager was still there. As she carefully pulled back a small piece of the curtain, the banging and screaming would start again, and she would run terrified back to the door sitting with her back resting on it, all the while shaking with fear, hoping that the manager wouldn't break through.

'When it went silent for the final time, I just sat there,' she said. 'I waited for an hour, then quietly went to the bedroom to get the duvet. I sat by the door, wrapped up in a sort of cocoon. I didn't sleep. It was the longest night of my life. I felt his presence all around me. I prayed for the morning to come and hoped that he wouldn't be there when it did.'

The next morning Helenna went to the local police station to file a complaint against her boss. To her utter surprise a complaint had already been filed against her, by the manager.

'He said that I'd been harassing him and was threatening to blackmail him! Luckily the police officer had treated it with the contempt it deserved and he listened to what I had to say. He was so supportive. I owe him a lot. He was the first person who had listened to me. Finally I felt sane again.'

Helenna's manager's behaviour is typical of the white-collar psychopath and illustrates a number of behavioural aspects that people are likely to face when encountering such individuals. One in particular is all too frequent and worrying – the potential for a shift to violence if things do not go their way. It also illustrates succinctly a vital aspect of psychopathy – the fact that the victim often feels that everything is their fault.

In Helenna's case, we can see that at the point where her manager realises that his world is threatened by one of his victims, he is prepared to do whatever it takes to destroy the threat – whether this be physical violence or psychological intimidation, or both.

The psychopath believes that they can only rely upon themselves in life to protect their own interests, and any method of protection is appropriate. As they become adults, they realise they may be punished by society for certain things. Because they are intelligent they develop strategies to avoid this punishment. This is not to say that they stop themselves from acting in a certain way because they believe it is wrong. They don't care that the behaviour is wrong – the only thing they truly care about is themselves and not getting caught.

Helenna's manager had been presented with the loss of

pleasure in his world as a result of her complaining to the regional manager. The psychopath's reaction is to immediately eliminate the threat. In organised crime this may be the elimination of a witness via the services of a hitman. In the world of Helenna it is through her psychological destruction.

If he can make her appear to be mad or having a nervous breakdown she becomes a less credible witness, and this, combined with his charming nature, will allow him to maintain his current position.

Helenna's emotional reactions to what has happened – her feeling like the world is spinning out of control, that what was happening was all her fault and even her questioning her sanity – are all common when related to the persistent attentions of a destructive psychopath.

Because the psychopath is often charming and manipulative, numerous victims we have counselled report that no one believes what they are saying about the offender, particularly when that person is in a position of authority or influence. Like Helenna, they feel that no one is listening to them and thus, after a while, they no longer think of themselves as being worthwhile. They feel as though maybe the psychopath, who continues to try and destroy them by making them feel like they are less than human, could actually be right. They are gradually being broken down, destroyed slowly from the inside and they often come to believe that it is they who cannot cope with life.

Like Helenna they begin to question why it is happening to them and wonder where the support system they always thought would be there for them actually is. They ask why the system and society isn't protecting them from what is happening and when they can't find answers they blame themselves, sometimes with devastating consequences.

Psychosomatic symptoms often manifest themselves in the victim. Many suffer nausea, diarrhoea, vomiting, trembling, stress reactions, dizziness, fainting, and a heightened startle reflex. They become fearful and mistrusting of others, develop a sense of isolation, and feel utterly powerless to stop the pain which is seemingly eating away their insides. Frequently they feel trapped by what is happening to them, and while they suffer, the psychopath continues to kill them mentally without remorse.

It transpired that Helenna's manager had treated his previous staff in a similar manner – hence the phone call to Helenna from her friend when she'd first been given the job. In the five years that the office had been functioning, six women had resigned from their positions, and almost all of them had filed official police complaints against the manager. Like Helenna, their complaints to the regional manager were brushed aside, which leads to the conclusion that the regional manager himself is not as perfect as his respectable position implies.

Looking at Helenna's case, it is easy to see that in the manager we have a definite psychopath. His actions were predictable. He was a cold-blooded, dishonest, exploitative, unprincipled and deceptive man. He was obsessed with power and control and relished putting Helenna 'in her place'. Helenna is sure that he particularly enjoyed making her life hell.

'I will never forget him laughing at me and the sting in his words when he found out that I'd complained about him,' she recalled. 'There was a sense of pure enjoyment in what he was doing, cold-hearted pleasure in the torment.'

Helenna is now rebuilding her life. Remarkably, and it is a testament to her strength of character and courage, her experience hasn't put her off working in the same field, nor in a similar office environment.

'As a victim, you try and get on with life,' she said. 'You try and remain composed and attempt to forget what has happened. But you can't. You are never the same person. The memories are always there. It is hard to forget.'

Lisa

Lisa is 36 years old. For the past seven years she has been working as a doctor. She is the victim of a white-collar psychopath. Here, she tells us how the experience has changed her life.

I've always thought of myself as being a strong and emotionally stable person. I was a confident child and knew from the age of six that I wanted to be a doctor – it was the only job I could imagine myself doing.

I worked hard through university and medical school and eventually qualified as a junior doctor in 1993. The work was tiring, the hours long, but every day was like a dream come true. I was doing something I was dedicated to, and I felt incredibly happy with my life.

Within a year I'd met and fallen in love with the most perfect man I had ever met. We were married 18 months later. My life had never been better. Shortly after my marriage I changed departments in the hospital I was working at and began duties in Accident & Emergency (A&E). This was a challenge that I felt able to meet and I was very excited about the future.

I knew as soon as I met Angela that she would be difficult to get on with. She was an A&E charge nurse and had been in the department for four years. There was no denying that she was good at her job, but her character and temperament were certainly suspect. Colleagues put her moodiness down to the fact that she was Irish, which I thought was ridiculous. To me she came across as being a bitter and twisted woman, for whatever reason, and I decided that I'd try and have as little to do with her as possible.

At first she seemed fine and despite my initial feelings about her, we actually got along well. It took her just four weeks to change that.

She started by openly questioning 90 per cent of my medical opinions and evaluations, not just in front of more junior staff, but also in front of patients. I had never before had my skills called into question or doubted, and it was quite shocking to be told I was wrong constantly by someone with less skill and clinical experience as myself.

Angela bullied me for over a year. She invented stories about me and spread rumours throughout the hospital about my personal and professional life. As you can imagine most of these were detrimental. Unbelievably, many of them were taken as being true.

Her mind games and psychological abuse towards me reached a point where it became impossible for me to concentrate solely on my job and the patients I was treating.

Whenever I attended someone in A&E, in the back of my mind I was wondering what the nurses and other doctors really thought about me and my skills. It made me a nervous wreck.

I fell pregnant at the about the same time as the abuse peaked. What should have been a period of joy for my husband and I turned into one of utter sadness and despair. Angela's actions had made me so nervous that I developed a rash that covered the whole of my back. I began to suffer from headaches, small ones at first, but these progressed to full blown and excruciating migraines. Initially I believed this was to do with my pregnancy and never imagined that it could be because of her.

She got worse, constantly picking on me, talking about me behind my back and that sort of thing. She'd move patient's charts so I couldn't find them. She would blatantly ignore me. Nobody would listen to my complaints. I felt like I was going mad.

Vomiting was a fairly regular occurrence for me. I couldn't keep anything down. I lost two kilos in weight in the space of a month despite being pregnant. I began to fear going to work. The night before I'd go back on duty after my rostered days off, I'd cry and cry. A black cloud would settle over me on the way to work. I began to hate what was happening to me and couldn't believe that nobody was on my side.

I suffered a miscarriage and lost my first child. I was devastated. I resigned from my post and have not been back to that hospital ever since. We moved shortly afterwards. It took me a year to pluck up the courage to go back to work.

I still suffer the headaches. I am no longer as confident as I used to be. My marriage has suffered as a result of what was done to me, but my husband and I are working hard to try and make everything work. The rash flares up now and again, especially when I am stressed or tired, which seems to be most of the time.

The scars, the majority of them mental, are still with me. Angela, a woman I pity, has made an indelible mark on my life. I want to rid myself of it. I am trying hard. But I fear her 13 months of mental torture could take me a lifetime to forget.

CHAPTER 8

Ripping off the World

Most of the crimes we have dealt with up until now have had a very physical element to them with an underlying threat of shocking violence.

But there is a crime that attracts a certain kind of criminal who doesn't need to be a menacing presence with a propensity for violence. This offender does not commit a physically terrifying crime, and his behaviour is often ignored by society and dismissed as being solely motivated by greed. This offender type does not spill his victim's blood. He is not a dark presence lurking in the shadows waiting to pounce. But he is devastating. He does cause trauma. He does cause loss.

We're talking about fraudsters – white-collar psychopaths with money on their minds. The cunning and conniving criminals that hit where many of us feel it hurts the most – in our pockets. The fraudster enters our world with his grand schemes and golden tongue, full of promises of wealth and status beyond our dreams. Just as quickly he leaves us with tattered bank accounts, fractured relationships and shattered dreams. We are left unsure as to how we let it all happen. We can't believe that we have been had. We repeatedly ask ourselves how we could have been so stupid to trust so much to someone we hardly knew and not see what it was they were doing.

It takes a certain kind of individual to commit fraud and in most cases people would find it hard to label these offenders as psychopathic. True, they are not bloodthirsty killers, or rapists living in a fantasy world. But they are ruthless. They are glib and superficial. They do believe they are more intelligent than everyone else. They are in it for themselves. They have no emotion or compassion for their victims. They are devils in suits with fast tongues.

As we already know, the above are all characteristics of a psychopath, according to Dr Hare's Psychopathy Checklist. So, are individuals who commit fraud truly psychopathic? To answer this question, let's take a look at the nature and scale of their crimes and the results of them on their victims.

Fraud is one of the most costly crimes to society. In Britain alone, JPMG Forensics puts the cost of fraud to the UK economy at between £13 billion and £16 billion every year. It is often suggested that when government bodies and large corporations are robbed of funds, by virtue of their size they can absorb the costs. But the cost of such fraud always finds its way down to the man in the street, leading to redundancies, price rises and possible tax increases. The community as a whole may be denied scarce resources, and vital services will be compromised.

Greed and opportunity are two factors that determine the extent of fraud. As the fifth largest economy in the world, the

UK provides a flourishing potential market for fraudsters. It's a paradox – the more economic growth there is, the more opportunity there is for the nation and its people to be ripped off. Success breeds crime. Crime breeds heartbreak and devastation.

Whether we have money or not, we are all potential victims. However, as is always the case, some sectors of society are more vulnerable to the threat. Sunil De Silva is a Crown Prosecutor. He is a veteran of fraud trials and deals with the aftermath of fraud almost every day.

'There are generally two types of fraud offender,' Sunil says. 'There are those fraudsters who target the greedy, and those who target the elderly. The greedy types are individuals who promise quick and supposedly high returns on a fixed investment, while those that prey on the elderly promise stable growth on investments that will provide healthy returns over the long term.'

In other words, fraudsters are similar to serial killers, rapists, stalkers and workplace bullies. They target the weak and the vulnerable, and they target them with a vengeance. They justify their actions as normal and necessary to earn a living and survive, in a cutthroat society where only the toughest survive.

'It's dog eat dog out there,' one convicted fraudster told us. 'You have to be able grab opportunities whenever they occur. That's all I did. I saw an opportunity, sized up the possibilities, found an audience and then went for it. What I did was nothing different from what is done on a daily basis by every other successful businessman. I made a profit from other people. Isn't that how society works?'

This type of offender has no problem whatsoever in justifying the hurt and misery his actions cause. These criminals see fraud as one of a number of mechanisms they can use to make their lives better by gaining both materially and financially. The making of easy money through fraud becomes a strategy, and the behaviour is repeated with new 'clients' being targeted or new scams being adopted.

Another key element seen in the fraud offender's behaviour is the fact that unlike the rest of us, who see their actions as clearly being wrong, the fraudster fails to see that he or she is doing wrong. These self-centred predators are without conscience. They truly believe that what they are doing is justified, because given half the chance, the rest of the population would do the same thing. In their eyes, we are all con artists – it's just that some of us are more courageous and daring in pulling off a scam than others are.

Fraud is much more than solely a way of getting other people's money – it also provides the offender with an opportunity to get back at society. We have been asked on many occasions whether a fraud offender feels any sense of satisfaction from knowing that he has financially ruined a person. The simple answer to this is yes, sometimes he does. In fact some fraudsters delight in the knowledge that they have permanently ruined someone, by virtue of them being more intelligent than the rest of society. It reconfirms their long-held belief that they possess superior levels of intelligence compared to everyone else. This in turn makes them feel good about themselves. To them, fraud is merely an easy way to make money. They don't care who gets hurt or ruined in the process.

A key factor which allows a psychopath to select the weakest possible victim is their total lack of emotional involvement in life – remember, to the psychopath, we (his potential targets) are mere objects who are begging to be exploited. A fraudster is no different. He or she is able to pick out a victim, then mould themselves into the person that victim wants them to be. The offender will listen intently to what the victim has to say and then say whatever that victim wants to hear. The fraudster, like the serial killer and the rapist before him, allows his victim to feel a sense of comfort with him. He uses his charm and glibness to ensure the smooth progression of the crime to meet his own selfish needs.

Elaborate schemes to obtain potential investors' money are always part of the plan, whatever the target audience. And the depth and nature of the scheme allows us to evaluate still further this offender's mind.

'Some fraudsters scrutinise the systems adopted by credit providers for any possible weak links,' says Sunil. 'For example, some credit providers seek to reduce inconvenience to genuine applicants by accepting telephone confirmation of information provided to them. Fraudsters have exploited this facility and dishonestly obtained large sums of money.

'You have to remember that these offenders are intelligent, have a thorough understanding of the financial markets and combine all of this with a ruthless and mean streak,' adds Sunil. 'Their scams are well thought out and meticulously planned. These scams will seem legitimate, the farthest thing from criminal activity a law-abiding member of the public will ever come across. But they are illegal. They are threatening.'

The fraudsters will not only be adept at setting up their scams, they will also be experts at promoting them and covering all of their tracks along the way to hide the illegality of the scam and their actions.

'Basically, fraudsters are common thieves,' says Sunil. 'They steal goods, services and money with impunity putting on a respectable front whenever it is needed, while maintaining their hidden ruthlessness all the way through.'

Engendering a belief in the victim that whatever it is they are involved in is legal is a critical ingredient of any successful fraud. As difficult as this might sound, to the fraudster it is easy, because he is greedy and he understands every aspect of this deadly sin. He knows all about the desire to make easy money – after all that's the reason he commits the offences he does. So, with all this knowledge on tap, it is a very easy task indeed to convince a stranger that what they are investing in is good and legal and that a small investment will turn into a huge windfall.

Convincing someone of the legality of a scheme is also easy – because the 'scheme' doesn't exist, but rather is a figment of the fraudster's criminal imagination. Because he is inventing the scheme, the act of adding comforting words and pieces of paper that help provide some reassurance to the victim, is easy. It's just another way in which this offender can feel good about himself, by displaying his superior intelligence.

When the fraud is carried out, victims are treated mercilessly. They are physically and mentally traumatised in much the same way as a victim of rape. Both types of offence are destructive, cruel and debilitating. In many cases that we have come across victims have suffered depression, insomnia, migraines, digestive problems, coronary problems, strokes, and anorexia. Suicides are common, as death is seen by the victim as being the only way to escape their newfound financial ruin.

The effects of fraud are felt for years to come. Lifestyle

changes are forced upon victims. Once comfortable lives are turned upside down. Houses are sold, possessions pawned in a bid to survive. Legal action is often fruitless. If the fraudster is caught, it's a fair bet that the money he or she has stolen will have been spent, either on a lavish lifestyle or paying off other debts. Quite often, the cost of a solicitor to fight a case is beyond the means of many victims of fraud. While some solicitors will accept payment on conviction of the offender, this is somewhat risky in many cases, as obtaining a guilty verdict in a fraud case is sometimes very difficult – thanks in large part to the offender's expert manipulation of the legal system.

'These people are well versed in playing the system,' comments Sunil. 'They use all of their manipulative skills to delay court proceedings, citing all sorts of legal and personal reasons for this. Frustratingly, they are sham artists of the highest order, and often get away with it.'

One police officer we talked to related a story of an offender who arrived at court groaning in pain and clasping his chest. Alongside him was a team of doctors and advisers, who informed the court that their client was suffering acute angina and that a guilty verdict would more than likely kill him. Not believing the story, the judge ordered that an independent doctor should conduct tests on the accused, to determine the veracity of the complaint.

'Even faced with this, the offender continued to manipulate the court,' the detective told us. 'He failed to turn up for the first medical examination, saying that he was too ill, and has still not been seen by the court appointed doctor. That was two years ago.'

This is typical behaviour. Fraudsters are chameleons. When free they have an ability to con and manipulate their way through society like no other offender type. The success of one fraud leads directly to the inception of another bigger scam. They learn that dishonesty pays, sometimes handsomely. They are pathological liars and they feel nothing for their victims. When caught, the false world they have built around them comes tumbling down. They have no desire whatsoever to come to terms with what they have done. Likewise they have no desire to take responsibility for their actions, and will do whatever they can to avoid being made to pay for their crime. It is at this moment that we see them display their true colours.

There are hundreds of fraud trials being conducted at any one time. Most will have been ongoing for months and may take many more months to conclude – all for the same reason. The fraudster, an expert liar, manipulator and cheat, is playing a game – a game of wits against the legal system, stalling trials and judgements in any way he can by claiming sickness, disability, temporary insanity or a host of other reasons why his trial cannot proceed. And it doesn't stop there. When the trial does begin and a guilty verdict is reached, the fraudster will beg for mercy, telling everyone in authority that he knows he has done wrong and is sorry for it. Don't be fooled. These individuals are not sorry for what they've done. They are only sorry that they have been caught. It is all a sham. They will cry. They will plead for forgiveness. They will con the authorities and parole boards into believing that they are redeemed. They have seen the error of their ways. Incredibly they will be believed and they will be set free – and when free they will find a new city, a new scam and a new set of victims to start all over again.

So, can we beat the fraudster? Yes, with the right resources. Compared to murder, sexual assault, robbery and burglary, fraud is given a relatively low priority. While there are specially trained teams of fraud investigators in all of the nation's police services, these teams are small in size and stretched beyond their limits. It would appear that the public perception of fraud as being a relatively minor crime, and one that poses a smaller threat to society than that of, say, armed robbery, is shared by the Establishment when it comes to the policing of it. Little money is spent on the necessary resources to investigate what are often complex fraud cases, and quite often, officers investigating an occurrence of fraud are sequestered to other investigations whenever they are needed. This leads to fraud cases taking months and even years to come to fruition. The challenge faced in investigating fraud in the 21st century lies in designing systems that allow the economy to flourish while blocking opportunities for fraud.

So, are fraudsters psychopaths? It is highly likely in most cases. We think they are the cream of all white-collar psychopaths. They are dangerous and more active than we probably care to imagine. They hurt and destroy people emotionally, mentally and financially. They are devils in suits that are hard to spot until it's too late, and as some cases prove they are costing the British taxpayer more than just billions of pounds every year – they are also wrecking lives and, at times, whole communities, in the process. This is demonstrated by one of the most widespread frauds of recent years.

Defrauding a State – The Western Australia Broking Scandal

It's a fraud so shocking in its scope that it defies belief. In all there are estimated to be around 7000 victims who have been ripped off to the tune of £100 million (AUD$300 million). It is a fraud case that didn't just affect Western Australia, where it is centred, but the whole of the country.

The story is a classic David and Goliath battle, with a cast of players and storyline worthy of Hollywood. In the one corner is a woman many victims refer to as their saviour. Denise Brailey, 53, is Australia's answer to Erin Brockovich, the real life crusader who was the inspiration for the hit Hollywood movie of the same name. Brailey, a single mother, is a former model with a dogged determination to uncover the truth. She works for a pittance from her housing commission unit in a Perth suburb, fighting for justice on behalf of thousands of defrauded investors, most of them elderly retirees.

Opposing her is a conspiracy of silence centred upon the State's broking industry – an industry riddled with corruption and deceit, which Brailey is slowly but surely uncovering.

The Western Australian Broking Scandal, as it has become known, first came into the media spotlight in 1997 following the establishment of the Real Estate Consumers' Association (RECA) by Brailey. RECA was set up to help victims of the real estate trade in Western Australia voice complaints about their brokers and settlement agents, many of whom it later turned out were defrauding clients of millions of dollars.

Brailey had gained notoriety for her rugged campaign to right a wrong done to her by the real estate industry, of which she was once a part.

'I had been selling real estate in the state and had been fleeced of $36,000 (the equivalent of £12,000) in commission by agents,' Brailey told us. 'I had three cases which I was pursuing in the courts. I eventually won one, the second, and had to abandon the third case as I ran out of money and couldn't afford to carry on. At the time I couldn't believe that they [the real estate industry] had treated one of their own so badly. I wondered how they would be treating the public. I then began to try and find out the depth of malpractice in the industry, as I suspected that there would be a lot, and do something to stop it. I wanted the State government to establish some sort of regulations for the industry.'

Within weeks of winning her case, other victims of the real estate industry were knocking on Brailey's door to ask for her help. At the time Brailey was studying for an Advanced Diploma in Accountancy, but she somehow managed to find the time to establish RECA. Twelve people, all victims of dubious real estate deals and all of them elderly retirees, turned up for the first meeting.

'By the end of the year we had 66 members,' says Brailey. 'This was a disgrace. It was obvious something was wrong. We had people turning up who had lost their homes as a result of shonky deals. Others had lost their life savings. I gathered all the cases, and went to the Ministry of Fair Trading and demanded that something be done to help these people. They completely ignored us.'

Brailey took the files containing all of the victim statements and case details to local Perth solicitor, Doug Solomon. Donating his time for free, Solomon took up the challenge and has since proven to be a major thorn in the side of the Western Australia government, which was toppled in a February 2001 election, some say on the back of Brailey and Solomon's work.

Brailey and Solomon have lifted the lid on what has to be one of the biggest and most astonishing fraud cases in history. Widespread mortgage and property fraud has left 7000 victims suffering combined losses which Brailey estimates to be at least £100 million. And that's just in Western Australia. Brailey also estimates that anything between £76 and £176 million has been fleeced in Queensland and that there could be as much as £0.5 billion gone missing throughout the whole of Australia. So far, Brailey has recovered £1.5 million through her own efforts.

'This has been a case of massive and high level white collar crime,' she says. 'We are seeing hundreds of millions of dollars changing hands in a matter of weeks. We don't know how much money has been siphoned off elsewhere out of the country, but we have uncovered cases of grand theft which means that this shifting of the money is going on.'

What has happened in Western Australia is a classic case of white-collar psychopathy gone mad. Unscrupulous real estate and mortgage agents have chanced upon a community which plays host to a high level of investment income, and a region in the midst of a building boom. With greed as their overriding motive, they have devastated this community and left a trail of bad debt and broken lives in their wake.

'We have had licensed brokers target elderly retirees who have large sums of newly acquired capital from superannuation, compensation payouts and disability dividends and so on,' comments Brailey. 'These traders were not fussy who they approached for funds. Usually they went for the 70 to 90 year olds, many of whom were people with little experience in investing money and no knowledge at all of the financial markets.'

Typically the brokers approached investors who responded to advertisements which offered above bank rate interest on safe and secure mortgage investments. The fact that solicitors would be drawing up the documentation and registering their interests on first mortgages only added to the victims' feelings of security regarding the potential investment. The scams were simple but effective, promising would-be investors competent, risk-free and secure investments where their capital would be as 'safe as houses' and the returns were, in some notable cases, guaranteed.

'In one case we had a property that was up for private sale in 1998 for offers of around £310,000,' explains Brailey. 'The couple who owned the property were retirees. They had rezoned the property and built some chalets on it for commercial use a decade earlier. They couldn't sell the property and the chalets were in a run down state. A smooth-talking, flashy gentleman broker arrived on their doorstep one day and offered them £500,000. They accepted. Twelve months went by and nothing happened. Eventually the purchase went through, and on the same day the broker and his lawyer raised a mortgage on the property for £800,000. The week before this, 60 retirees had answered an ad in the newspaper, which touted the property as a viable business venture that had recently been valued at £1 million. The retirees were asked to contribute towards a pooled first mortgage which represented a 65 per cent loan to value ratio. They were not told that in reality the loan represented a huge 300 per cent mortgage. Many of them responded positively and invested their money. All of them lost out. After 12 months without income and supporting legal bills, they suffered an average 70 per cent loss of their capital, plus interests, plus costs. The property sold at auction in December 2000 for £250,000. That's a typical scam and one we've seen repeated too many times to mention.'

The offenders, and so far there have been a number of convictions, are all well-heeled, smooth-talking businessmen with a taste for expensive cars and equally expensive private schools for their children. They are the very essence of what is termed a white-collar criminal. It is difficult, legally at any rate, to say whether they are psychopathic, but a number of behavioural characteristics which are common in psychopaths have been exhibited by these greedy conmen.

Without fail, the offenders Denise Brailey has come across have been charming, suave, sophisticated, glib and superficial. All of them have a grandiose sense of self-worth and have shown no remorse when confronted with their crimes.

'From my experience of them they have proved themselves to be incapable of feeling sorry for anyone but themselves,' she says. 'Some of them have laid the blame for what happened on the investors. One of them has even gone so far as to call the investors "an ungrateful lot". They blame the victims.'

This shifting of the blame is typical of a psychopathic offender. They do not want to face the consequences of their actions, or take any responsibility for the devastation they have caused. Their only interest is self-preservation. In fact, it is usual for the offender to apportion the majority of the blame to the victim. They justify this by believing that it is the victim's lack of intelligence and common sense that has led to them becoming a victim. All the offender was doing, in his mind, was his job.

'One particular broker, who stole around £1.75 million, said in court that what happened was "just a case of mismanagement",' says Brailey. 'He believed that if the investors had kept quiet he could have repaid them from the accounts of other investors who were signed up with him. He'd kept a similar house of cards standing for over eight years. When the defaulting loans started to escalate, the complaints to the Office of Fair Trading reached a peak, and the media and I besieged the broker constantly, the world collapsed around him.'

As if the loss of £100 million and the shattered dreams and lives this has brought with it isn't enough, there has been an even more tragic fallout as a result of the massive fraud.

'We have lost 38 people since this started,' reveals Brailey. 'Most of them are men and they have died of illnesses that I believe are related to the pressures and stresses they have been forced to live under as a result of this criminal activity. It is terribly sad and makes me angry that all of this has been allowed to happen.'

While the focus of attention has been firmly fixed on Westurn Australia, other states and even more innocent victims could soon be feeling the impact of this fraudulent activity. According to Brailey and a number of other sources, many of the brokers charged and already convicted of offences relating to the broking scandal had business and social contacts throughout Australia.

'At RECA alone, we have 500 victims on our books from

Queensland, at least 20 from Tasmania and many more besides from New South Wales, South Australia and the Northern Territory,' she says. 'The whole country will be affected by this. According to our surveys a staggering 40 per cent of retirees are currently in need of income assistance, and if compensation is not paid, these individuals will be entitled to Government support for the rest of their lives. We are seeing previously self-funded retirees seeking pensions and health care cards in order to survive. These are people who, had nothing happened, would never have been a burden on society. The Government is facing a £704 million budget blowout over the next decade as a result of what has happened in Western Australia. In time, we will all pay the cost of this massive fraudulent activity.'

Another disturbing possibility that could impact society in years to come is the fact that there are many more criminally minded brokers out there who have not been convicted of an offence yet and who are this very day investing other people's money into a new breed of frauds.

'This is a major concern,' says Brailey. 'Traders are now streetwise to the method of detection. Some of those who were involved in pooled mortgage scams have shut down their businesses and moved. They have refined their schemes and are now starting new scams on unsuspecting middle-aged investors.'

How we find these psychopaths amongst us and stop them is a challenge we all now face. It is a challenge we have to address if we are to maintain order in society.

CHAPTER 9

The Pain of Loss

I t's in their eyes where you see the turmoil the most and it is this aspect that attracts your attention and, for want of a better word, sorrow. Eyes without sparkle, eyes that have lost their will to see the beauty and the good in the world. Eyes often without a sense of hope.

While much has been written and said about the chilling, black eyes of psychopaths over the years, in this instance we are not talking about their eyes, but rather those of their often forgotten victims – the surviving family members, friends and relatives of the psychopath's murderous actions. The parents, brothers, sisters, wives, husbands, sons and daughters of murder victims. Individuals who have all shared the ultimate loss, and live with their grief forever embedded deep within their hearts and souls.

Many of us have experienced the death of a close family member. While some of these deaths may well be unexpected, and some expected – considering the age and relative health of the deceased – the vast majority are not malicious deaths. They are either accidental or natural. Without fail there is no intent to cause death. It is simply a sad fact of life that we cannot live forever and when our time is up there is nothing we can do about it.

Families can grieve for their deceased relative. Over time they can come to terms with the death of a loved one, and bring some sense of normality back into their lives. But this is not the case for those families who are touched by a psychopath.

For them life is never the same again. They live with the knowledge that their loved one died as a result of a wilful decision by another human being to take their life. They live with the knowledge that their relative suffered, and may have been in terrible pain at the time of their death. They know that their loved one died alone, and at their hour of greatest need, they were not there to help them. They live with the knowledge that they will never find an answer as to why their loved one was chosen by a murderer. They will spend the rest of their lives asking why it happened – perhaps even blaming themselves for not doing enough to protect their relative. They will live their lives like this, all the while wondering why this devastation and heartbreak had to visit them.

The focus of this book is on psychopaths and why they do what they do. In writing it, we have tried our best throughout to give you, the reader, a glimpse inside the psychopath's mind. However, notwithstanding this being the case, we felt it was only right to show you the full impact of their actions. In clinical work as well as writing and researching *Psychopaths* we have come across some incredibly brave and courageous people. Many times these people have been the direct victim of a psychopath, such as a rapist, stalker or former work colleague. These are individuals who face seemingly insurmountable problems and life changes on a daily basis. Their lives have been forever changed by their experiences and they are often shadows of their former selves.

While much attention is rightly focused on the people who lose their lives at the hands of a psychopath and the horrible crimes that have been committed against their person, there are many more victims of psychopaths who are not necessarily the direct physical target of the offender. These are the people we will focus on in this chapter – the surviving relatives and families of murder victims.

There are a number of support groups and agencies which provide assistance, help and advice to the families of murder victims. Their tireless efforts often go unnoticed by the general public, but their work helps to heal wounds that are hard to heal. Every day, and unfortunately in an increasing number of occasions as a result of the violent society we live in, they prove to be a lifeline for families in what must surely be their longest, and most desperate, hour of need.

In order to get an idea of just how great the impact of serial murder has on a victim's family, I travelled to Sydney, Australia where out of the consequences of a terrible tragedy, a unique and vital resource has been set up to combat the effects of these hideous crimes.

Situated in a nondescript tower block in the heart of Sydney are the offices of the Homicide Victims Support Group (HVSG) of New South Wales. The group offers counselling and support services for families and friends of murder victims and currently looks after some 800 families throughout the state.

The HVSG was formed in 1993 by the parents of murder victims Anita Cobby and Ebony Simpson, along with grief counsellors at Glebe Morgue. Its founders believed that not enough was being done for the families of murder victims, both in terms of the level of support provided and in the way their interests were looked after and protected by the law. As well as providing help, advice and a shoulder to cry on, the group also makes its presence felt with regard to legislative issues. Over the years the group has lobbied for changes to over 140 pieces of legislation. It has been credited with the creation of the Victims' Rights Charter, the introduction of a DNA database in New South Wales, and the establishment of victims' registers. It has given victims a voice – and it is one that the Establishment cannot fail to hear.

Alex Faraguna is one of the four full-time counsellors employed by the HVSG. She knows all about the pain and emotional turmoil families of murder victims endure, as she is in daily contact with them and is often one of the first counsellors to meet with the families in the days following a murder.

'All of our cases are referred to us by the police,' says Alex, a softly spoken Englishwoman who has worked with the HVSG for three years. 'We then go to the family's home and let them know about what we do, detail the services we offer and talk to them about what has gone on and the legal processes that are occurring.'

There are many stages of grief and despair that the families and friends of murder victims go through following their relative's murder. Shock and numbness are common. A sense of bewilderment that there are people out there in society who can be so evil as to brutally take a life consumes the relatives. Anger and the need for vengeance and justice are common desires.

'Everyone is different and reactions vary depending on how close the person was to the murder victim,' says Alex. 'However, many people do experience the same emotions and have similar reactions to the murder.'

The first feeling is a strong sense of disbelief. Relatives find it hard to believe that their loved one has been taken away from them. They feel it must be a mistake. The police have got it wrong, it is not their family member or friend that is dead, but somebody else's. 'The truth is so terrible that they don't want to believe it,' comments Alex.

Then comes the shock. It encompasses the body, numbing the system to what has happened, giving the grieving relative the feeling that their body has shut down. The shock of what has happened can last for weeks, sometimes resurfacing months after the initial event. A deep sense of sadness, like a grey fog engulfing the soul, follows the shock. This is the time when tears are shed, and the question why is asked.

According to Alex, this stage of emotional turmoil is reached some three to four weeks after the murder. The victim's relatives and friends hit a wall – they become extremely sad and they shift between feeling numb and upset to feeling bitter and angry.

The shedding of tears is a positive first step on the road to recovery, however. Scientific research has shown that tears heal – each tiny drop contains chemicals which, when released and allowed to flow, reduce stress, anxiety and pain. A further positive step is taken by talking about the tragedy and personal loss with a counsellor such as Alex.

'There's very little benefit in keeping things bottled up and churning around inside,' she says. 'The victims are worth every tear shed and emotion expressed and this phase is a crucial one in helping those left behind come to terms with their loss.'

Feelings of anger and rage accompany the shock and numbness. Like the tears, many people try to keep their anger and hatred towards the offender contained within themselves. This, however, could lead to problems further down the line.

'All the tension that is building up inside a person needs to be released and dealt with early,' Alex says. 'If not, it could resurface in another way at another time, perhaps with other family members or colleagues. This could lead to problems with relationships and so on. It is far better and easier in the long term to talk about feelings and emotions early on, and that is what we try to encourage. Basically we are there for the families to act as their sounding boards. We can help them address their emotions and prevent them from hurting themselves and others close to them mentally in the weeks, months and years that follow.'

Another emotional reaction suffered as the result of a psychopath's murderous act is that of guilt. As well as asking themselves why what's happened has happened to one of their loved ones, relatives and friends of the victim commonly ask themselves what if?

'There is an incredible feeling of guilt and blame for the incident,' Alex confides. 'Close family members, especially older brothers and sisters, continually go over details leading up to the murder and question their actions and behaviour. Inevitably, they end up blaming themselves for not being there when their sibling needed them the most. It is one of the saddest aspects of the job.'

The psychopath's diabolical impact is felt physically as well. Sleepless nights are common and when relatives and friends of murder victims – as well as surviving victims of psychopaths – finally do manage to get some rest they invariably suffer nightmares. Fatigue is common, and many people complain of feeling constantly exhausted or generally tired or unwell. Many victims find themselves feeling lethargic and unable to do things because they cannot be physically bothered. Others, however, find they become hyperactive and are unable to find the time to relax and take a break from what they are doing.

Health problems are common too. Victims suffer from frequent colds, headaches, digestive problems, nausea and a host of muscular aches and pains. Some choose to relieve their stress by overeating, while others lose their appetites altogether, compounding the problems associated with low energy levels and disturbed sleeping patterns.

Arguments between partners are also common. 'Men and women have different ways of dealing with their grief,' comments Alex. 'We find that men prefer to keep their emotions inside and spend their time doing physical things to take their mind off what has happened. Women, on the other hand, are more likely to let their emotions out and tend to want to talk more openly about what has happened. We find that some couples find it hard to understand their other half's reactions to the murder. While one cries, the other shuts down.'

This difference between the sexes often causes irreparable damage. Sadly, around 80 per cent of marriages fall apart following a murder of a loved one. It is yet another terrible consequence of the actions of the psychopath.

Of course, none of this goes through the psychopath's mind when he is committing his offence. He doesn't care about what happens to the victim's family after the crime, in the same way that he doesn't care what happens to his victim. All he cares about is himself – after all, as we know, he has a complete lack of emotion, is self-serving and has little grasp of what is right or wrong.

The victims and their families are the last thing on these offenders' minds. The psychopath lives for the moment when he can have complete power and control over something he perceives as weaker and more vulnerable than himself. It is a moment that he fantasises about and plans for days, weeks or maybe even months. It is a moment that becomes the central theme and focus of his life. The psychopath hopes the reality will live up, in some way, to his demented fantasies. If it doesn't, then he will simply try again and again, until it does. That is what makes the offender so abhorrent.

Headstones are all that remain of many of the psychopath's victims. For them, the pain is over. They are in a better place. But for those left behind, life is never the same again. Time does not heal the awful memories that a psychopath inflicts. Their impact is felt for generations to come. The survivors live their lives having been touched by the devil. It is a touch, that is fleeting, but lethal, and it lasts forever.

Anita Cobby

It was undoubtedly one of Australia's most brutal murders. One that now, over 15 years later, still shocks to the core. A murder so savage and terrifying that it is impossible to even try to comprehend what could possibly have driven five men to destroy a beautiful woman with her whole life ahead of her in such a barbaric way.

Anita Cobby finished the final nursing shift of her life at Sydney Hospital in Macquarie Street, on the evening of Sunday, February 2, 1986. It had been a routine day's work for the attractive 26-year-old, and upon finishing it she'd gone for a meal with friends at one of her favourite Lebanese restaurants in nearby Redfern. After finishing her meal, Anita was driven to Central Station by one of her dining companions and at roughly 8.45pm caught a train heading to Blacktown. She arrived less than 30 minutes later and began the 20-minute walk to her parent's house in Sullivan Street, where she'd been staying for the previous six weeks after splitting up from her husband, fellow nurse John Cobby. She never made it home.

As Anita walked along Newton Road, a stolen Holden Commodore containing five men drove past her. One of the men, 19-year-old John Travers, had caught a glimpse of Anita as they drove by. He ordered the driver of the car, Mick Murphy, 34, to turn around and pull up beside her. Murphy obeyed. As the car approached Anita the second time, Travers and the third member of the pack, Michael Murdoch, also aged 19, got out and stood in front of her. They made a grab for Anita's handbag. The young nurse fought them off, determined to prevent the thugs from taking her bag. The scuffle lasted for less than a minute until Anita, calling out for help, was manhandled into the back of the car, and pushed down on to the floor before the vehicle sped away.

Within seconds of being forced into the vehicle, Anita Cobby was stripped of her clothes and beaten. After stopping for petrol at a local service station – paying for the fuel using money stolen from Anita's purse – the car headed towards nearby Prospect. On the way Anita was raped by Murdoch and Travers, while the other gang members, Les and Gary Murphy (the younger brothers of Mick Murphy, the driver) looked on and cheered their encouragement.

The Commodore eventually came to a halt next to an empty paddock in Reen Road, Prospect. Dragged out of the car by her hair, Anita was gang raped. All five men took it in turn to brutally assault her ravaged body. Not content with this, the men beat Anita again, before anally raping her and forcing her to perform oral sex.

Begging for mercy and lapsing into unconsciousness, Anita was dragged through a barbed wire fence by her hair and dumped on the spot where she would eventually die and mercifully escape the onslaught of the animals that had captured her. But Travers, Murdoch and the Murphy brothers had not done with her yet. No longer able to resist, and Anita had fought for her life all the way, she was raped one more time by Mick Murphy, who then proceeded to kick and beat her repeatedly about the head and upper body, completely disfiguring her once eye-catching face.

Leaving her crumpled and violated body in the paddock, the five men went back to the car. However Travers was worried. He believed that Anita had seen his face, and would be able to recognise the distinctive teardrop tattoo under his left eye. He decided that there was only one course of action to take. Anita Cobby must die. Urged on by the others, Travers, knife in hand, walked calmly back to where Anita lay face down in a growing pool of blood. Sitting on her back, he pulled her head up by the hair and with brutal force slit her throat twice, covering himself with her blood in the process as Anita breathed her last breath. The force of the knife cuts on her throat was enough to almost decapitate her. Anita Cobby was dead.

When Anita's body was found, detectives called to the scene could hardly believe their eyes. Trails of blood marked the route that Anita had been dragged along. Pieces of her flesh and hair dotted the surrounding area. Her body had been almost completely drained of blood, so severe was the attack.

Garry and Grace Lynch are Anita's parents. They have lived for the past 15 years knowing that their daughter was murdered in the shocking manner just described. They have lived knowing that their precious and talented daughter died an agonising death. They know she suffered. They know the five men who killed her showed Anita no mercy. Their lives have been touched not by one devil, but by five. Their pain is intense, it touches you when you meet them and when you hear them speak of Anita and remember that horrific moment in their lives.

But somehow this brave couple have survived. They are a living example to anyone that has lost a relative to murder, that there is hope – lives can be put back together. They are respected, revered even. Speaking to them you get a sense of how special their daughter was. Anita would be proud of them, as their other daughter Kathryn is proud of them. Their fortitude and faith is almost tangible. They are strong, dignified and courageous. This is part of the story of how they have survived:

GRACE: When Anita didn't come home that night we didn't think anything of it. She was 26, had travelled around the world and was as independent and worldly wise as you'd expect of someone who worked in the profession she did. She did tell us that she might be late home on the Sunday as she was going for a meal, so when she didn't come home I assumed she'd stayed with her friends as she sometimes did.

GARRY: We got a phone call early Monday afternoon from Sydney Hospital. They told us that Anita hadn't shown up for work. My heart sank. We'd heard nothing from her, which was completely out of character. So I went and reported her missing to the police. We didn't know what had happened until Tuesday, when the detectives came and knocked on the door.

GRACE: The police told Garry on the front lawn. I knew something terrible had happened but couldn't bring myself to admit that Anita might be dead. Garry told me a couple of minutes later. We didn't know how she'd died, or what had happened to her. All we knew was that her body had been found in a paddock somewhere.

GARRY: I was taken to the morgue to identify her. Grace wanted to come with me but the detective advised her not too. Driving there I asked whether Anita had been violated and beaten. They told me yes. They told me she was in a state. I didn't know she'd had her throat cut until I heard it reported on the news. When I saw her at the morgue she was wearing a high lace collar that was buttoned up to her chin. You couldn't see the marks. I suppose they dressed her like that to save us the shock of seeing her throat. Her face had been battered. One of her eyes was destroyed, all puckered and bruised. Her teeth had been knocked out. Yet even so she looked beautiful. She looked at peace. Beautiful, despite all those terrible things they'd done to her.

GRACE: I lived through what I imagined Anita went through in the last two hours of her life over and over in my mind. I imagined all sorts of things happening to her. I felt utterly devastated. I didn't believe that anyone could be as devastated as me. Of course, I know now that people are and will be in the future, but at that moment, it was horrific. The sadness, the disbelief, it was devastating.

GARRY: The police took me to where Anita had died. A local farmer found her body. Apparently he'd noticed his cows milling around in a circle in the paddock and wondered what was wrong. He went back a couple of hours later and the cows were still milling around. He thought it was odd, went over to see what was the matter and found Anita. The cows were licking the blood off her body.

The discovery of Anita's body immediately thrust the Lynches into the media spotlight. Within hours, details of Anita's death were being sent around the country and the world. Lurid newspaper headlines played on the gory nature of her death. Garry became the spokesperson for the family.

GARRY: Our lives changed from that moment on. We'd lost someone precious to us and then were thrust into the media spotlight. The very public nature of Anita's death was difficult to deal with. I was pushed into giving interviews. We didn't really want any of that. It was the kind of notoriety you would never wish to have.

GRACE: Most of the media were very good and understood the pain we were going through. We didn't want to come across as always crying our eyes out. I didn't want that. Anita wouldn't have wanted us to behave like that.

GARRY: We kept it together. When the media went away and we were alone as a family, we mourned Anita in our own way. We were all incredibly shocked by what had happened. It was totally devastating for everyone concerned.

GRACE: At the very beginning it was really horrific trying to cope. You wonder why something like this has to happen to you. You ask why someone close to you had to be murdered. You try to find reasons, answers to why. You listen to the radio and watch the TV and you realise that the family, the girl they are talking about in the news is you. It's your daughter. It's hard to handle. Hard to come to terms with.

GARRY: When they arrested Travers and his gang, we were hugely relieved. Delighted that they had been caught and wouldn't have the chance to hurt anyone else. We didn't see Travers at the trial as he had already pleaded guilty, but we saw the other four. They looked as if they couldn't care less about what they'd done. They showed no emotion, had no compassion. It was very difficult to see. None of them showed any remorse. If anybody in this world was psychopathic, it was those four cowards.

GRACE: After the trial we went back to work and tried to get on with our lives. You learn to live with your loss. You have to, otherwise you'd fall apart. As time goes by the horrific part of what has happened gradually fades. The murder isn't something that is constantly on your mind like it is in the early days. You move on.

GARRY: You put it behind you. Sure there's been tears and sobbing. But for me, I've put what happened into my back pocket and every now and again I pull it out. I have my little moment of grief, then I put it away again. It's not something you can carry with you in the open all of the time. You have to put it behind you. There's a realisation that you mustn't let the grief and sadness drag you down. We have another daughter. She doesn't want to see us as sobbing wrecks, crying and sad all of the time.

Hate is a strong word for many people. In the ordinary world, genuinely deep hatred for another human being is very rarely felt. With what happened to their daughter, Garry and Grace had a pretty good excuse to hate Travers, Murdoch and the Murphy brothers. In what is surely a testament to their strength and depth of character, they feel no hate towards their daughter's murderers.

GARRY: Hate is a waste of time. I don't hate them. At the time, we poured all our thoughts into our daughter. We didn't want to waste our emotions on those five animals.

What I did was dismiss them. I have dismissed them from my life as being human and sane. They're ignorant minds.

GRACE: You can't afford to live your life hating someone or something. We are not like the five. We are aware of a finer principle for living and endeavour to follow that principle. We've got our faith in God, we have a family to think about. We have a daughter and very young grandchildren who don't want to see us full of hate. Anita wouldn't want us to be full of hate.

Anita's murder changed the Lynches' lives. Their family unit was destroyed, yet somehow they managed to survive.

GRACE: We have definitely changed. We've become more caring. We've tried to help other people who've survived a murder. We've relied on our faith and our belief in God to get us through some tough times.

GARRY: We've always had a strong belief in God and that has certainly helped us through what's happened. We believe she's still with us, with Jesus, in another reality. We feel that she's close to us, looking over us. One day we'll see her again in that other reality, but for now, we have no place there, we can't intrude. We have to wait our turn.

GRACE: We're not grieving any more. You can't spend the rest of your life living like that and I know that Anita wouldn't want us to be like that either. Going over all of the whys doesn't help one bit. You have to move on, come to terms with what's happened and accept it.

GARRY: Sometimes we think how Anita's life would have

panned out had she not been taken when she was. She was a free soul, an exceptionally good person, a good nurse, a loving daughter and sister. At the time of her death she was just working out her life, discovering what she wanted to do and where she wanted to be. It was a terrible fate what happened. A terrible thing to have happened to someone so loving and beautiful.

GRACE: As time goes on you learn to live without them. I miss having Anita to talk to, miss having her near. That loss will never go away. She's in a special place now, where her memory is revered.

We're not sure that the Lynches have become more caring. Having sat with them in their neat house we're convinced that they have always been caring people – their compassion for others didn't come about as a result of their daughter's death. This caring nature has always been there. It has always been a facet of their relationships, their family life. They have always been the kind of people who would do anything to help their fellow man in his hour of need. It makes the loss of Anita, from such a warm, loving and caring family, all the more tragic.

Anita, or at least a part of her, lives on however. A legacy of her death is the Homicide Victims' Support Group, of which Garry Lynch was a founding member. As a result, Garry and Grace Lynch have helped others cope with their losses and rebuild their lives. Alex Faraguna is one of many people who has nothing but admiration and respect for them.

'They are the sweetest and bravest people you're likely to meet,' she says. 'They've suffered something that is hard to imagine, yet they have managed to keep themselves together and given so much of themselves to others. They are a remarkable couple.'

CHAPTER 10

The Problems We Face

There are many things we know and understand about psychopaths, and hopefully *Psychopaths* has helped you to learn more about these monsters amongst us.

For a start we know these types of people are out there (between 3 and 5 per cent of the adult male population), and that there are a high number of them living free alongside each and every one of us. We know how dangerous they are and can be, and we know the threat posed to society by their actions. We know that no matter who we are, where we live, or what we do, we are all potential victims of the psychopath.

We know how the psychopath's mind works. We know, through research and clinical study, how these devils think. We also know how to get inside their heads and predict their likely behaviour and development – we have done it in this book.

But do we know how to beat them? Do we know how to minimise the risk of being a victim? Do we know how to identify them before it's too late? Do we know how to expose them once they have embarked on their devastating campaigns? Once captured, can they be changed?

Thankfully, the answer to most of these questions is yes. However, before we can even begin to address the issue of fighting back, we have to first comprehend the extent of the problems we face. We have to fully understand the reasons for the terror of the psychopath. We have to know exactly what it is we are dealing with.

We know that the psychopath is driven by a desperate need for power, domination and control. No matter whether the psychopath is a serial killer or a stalker, dressed in scruffy jeans or a designer suit, his or her needs are always the same. But are they mad, or just plain bad, these devils in society? The answer is as complex as the subject matter it covers.

The Macquarie Dictionary partially defines 'mad' as being disordered in intellect or insane. This definition certainly applies to the majority of the psychopathic individuals we have encountered in this book. Their actions are hard to fathom, almost beyond belief. Surely only a madman would hunt, terrorise, assault or kill a fellow human being?

Legally however, the psychopath is considered as being far from insane. In fact they are dealt with as being the exact opposite. They are considered sane. How, we are often asked, can this be? The answer is simple. Take a look at the psychopath's crimes. Think for a moment about the extent to which these individuals plan and fantasise about their acts. Think about how they carry out their crimes and scams. Even the smallest and what appear to be most insignificant aspects of the crime are planned out in intricate detail. Nothing is left to chance. The right weapons, the right tools, the right words and actions are all used and factored into the crime in order for it to be pulled off as smoothly as possible. And all along, despite their lack of emotion and personalities, the psychopath knows that what he or she is doing is wrong. Only a sane mind thinks this way, and as such they can be held legally responsible for their actions. It is vital that we understand that these sick and twisted individuals do have control over what they do. In committing their acts, they simply ignore society's rules. They ignore the law. They please themselves. They know what they are doing is wrong – after all you would never see a psychopath attempt to kill or rape someone in front of a police officer, would you?

If you're still not convinced that these people are sane, then think about their behaviour immediately following the offence. Often they go to elaborate lengths to remove evidence from the scene. Think about the organised serial killer. The very word 'organised' tells us something as to the state of his mind. When caught, many psychopathic offenders try to blame their actions not on themselves, but rather on some mental illness that afflicts them. They will claim that they are suffering from a multiple personality disorder and that they had no recollection of what they had done. They will blame others for their actions, citing the sexual abuse they suffered as a child as a reason for their brutal crimes. They will claim voices told them to kill, or that God Himself was their tutor. It takes a sane mind to even think up such things on short notice – a sane and expertly manipulative mind. That is why, more often than not, their outlandish claims are dismissed as being totally false and mere attempts by them to escape just punishment for their crimes.

The white-collar psychopath is even more interesting. Here is a fundamentally very intelligent person committing an act that they know is clearly wrong and devastating to others, yet they are rarely, if ever, found out and brought to justice. As a result of this non-capture, they are never made to feel responsible for their actions. Don't for a moment think that they are not aware of this. They are. It is what drives them on. It is the reason why they increase the level and occurrence of their destructive behaviour. They make a conscious decision to escalate their behaviour, or even change whatever they do slightly to make their campaigns more efficient in order to increase the pain and suffering caused, allowing them to enjoy an even greater sense of power and control. Here is another conclusive example of the sanity of the psychopath. Could you imagine for a moment an insane individual exhibiting such behavioural characteristics?

Looking at this issue from a purely psychiatric perspective of whether psychopaths are mad or bad, it is certainly clear that these individuals have a definites personality disorder. The American Psychiatric Association defines this as 'a pervasive pattern of disregard for and violation of the rights of others that begins in early childhood and continues on into adulthood'.

For sure, the psychopath does lack a number of fundamental characteristics that make the majority of the population law abiding and empathetic. In addition, the psychopath also displays different thought processes compared to the rest of us. However, don't be fooled. These differences confirm that it is the psychopath himself who chooses to do what he does as opposed to having voices in his head or visions playing out before him that impel him to kill, rape, stalk, terrorise and defraud.

Is madness a lack of control over behaviour or a lack of fundamental human characteristics that most of us share? That is for you, the reader to decide. Whatever answer you arrive at depends entirely on your perspective. What doesn't however, is the fact that these individuals, these psychopaths, are abnormal. They are human aberrations. But legally they are not insane.

It's all well and good talking about the impact of psychopaths on our lives. But can we actually do something to stop them? Can we discover them at an early age and stop the psychopathic pattern of character development in its tracks before they have a chance to mature and cause harm?

Throughout *Psychopaths*, we have shown the development of the psychopath from a psychological viewpoint in order to provide you with some understanding of both how their minds work and why they come to think the way they do. These aspects of the psychopath's persona are developed early on in childhood. Quite often, psychopathic development and maturity can be seen to be taking place in a child who demonstrates a number of certain behavioural patterns. If witnessed and experienced these childhood traits can be cause for alarm and should be addressed. It must be remembered, however, that just because a child displays some of these symptoms doesn't necessarily mean that they will become a psychopath in later years. We have included the characteristics merely to provide parents, teachers and counsellors, as well as the community at large, with a checklist of character traits that if seen together may indicate a possible future problem child.

Any child that exhibits the homicidal triad previously discussed – cruelty to animals, fascination with or setting of fires, and enuresis (bed-wetting) after an inappropriate age (above nine years old) – is certainly a major cause for concern and should be addressed urgently.

A child displaying the above patterns of behaviour has the potential to become a future serial killer or sexual homicide offender. If the same child is withdrawn or socially isolated, prone to long bouts of daydreaming, claims that they feel out of place in society, and has been sexually, physically or mentally abused the risk factor of future dangerousness is increased.

The American Psychiatric Association provides a number of other behaviour patterns that should cause concern if observed in a child. These include bullying, threatening or intimidating others, initiating physical fights, destroying property, motor vehicle theft, running away, truancy, and finally conning or lying to other people repeatedly. According to the Diagnostic and Statistical Manual of Mental Disorders – 4th edition (DSM–IV) these behaviours must be severe and present to such an extent that they cause impairment in social, academic or occupational environments. These types of characteristics can develop during early childhood or adolescence. They can be classified as being mild, moderate or severe, depending upon the extent to which they are exhibited, and provide possible pointers as to future anti-social personality disorder or psychopathy.

While the above characteristics are extremely helpful in facilitating experts to uncover possible future psychopaths, a much more important part of the early identification process is the ability to understand the attitude of the child itself. Specialists, such as psychologists and psychiatrists, will routinely look at the way the child acts and reacts to the world around it. Is the child withdrawn? Does the child feel entitled to anything it wants? Will the child do whatever it takes to get what it wants? Is the child intelligent? Does the child disregard the rights of others or perhaps even deliberately violate the rights of others? Does the child respond well to punishment or any other technique that is aimed at modifying its behaviour? Does the child bully others, lie, cheat or steal? Is the child constantly in trouble at school? The answers to these questions are vital if we want to uncover the child's core personality and address the possibility of future destructive behaviour. A parent, teacher or counsellor that can answer yes to any of the questions above should think seriously about obtaining help and advice from a suitably qualified professional.

But what about the child who outwardly exhibits none of the above, yet somehow, for whatever reason, doesn't seem quite right? In our experience, it is this type of child that is often the most worrying and potentially the most dangerous. Already, very early on, they have learnt to camouflage their acts and thoughts. They have learnt how to get away with things. This is a skill. A skill of cunning and deceit that could lead to much more devastating behaviour later on.

Think carefully, however, before you label a child as one that may be problematic and may be even dangerous in years to come. There are a number of independent psychological disorders that may be easily confused with the behaviour patterns described here. For this reason, only suitably qualified psychologists or psychiatrists should undertake detailed psychological character assessments on the young. This avoids the inherent dangers associated with incorrectly labelling an innocent child as a future potential psychopath.

Left unchecked the child may grow into the kind of offender we have read about earlier: the Glovers, Traverses, Leonskis, Gacys, Bundys and Dahmers of the world. They blaze their way through society destroying whatever is in their path. When they are loose, is it possible to spot them in time to prevent yourself from being the next victim? Unfortunately, while there are characteristics you can remain alert for, there is very little you can do to protect yourself from these raging monsters.

Why is this the case? Simply put the reason you can't protect yourself, except for the obvious personal security measures you can take to minimise your risk of becoming a victim, is because the psychopath doesn't rationalise his thoughts like you. He is on an altogether different plain. Their thought processes are not necessarily constrained by social standards. They know what they want from you. They know how to get what they want from you and they will do anything to get it – things that are far beyond the realms of your imagination. And they are so good at doing this that you won't realise you are a victim until the moment of the attack or, in the case of white-collar psychopaths such as fraudsters, maybe months or even years afterwards.

It's not all hopeless however. There are a number of things you can do to lower your potential risk of becoming a victim. These strategies, many of which will be discussed in greater detail in the next chapter, do not guarantee your personal safety, but they are the best on offer.

The psychopath's act essentially revolves around a number of key behavioural phases, namely the contact, manipulation, kill and victim phases. You can employ a number of defensive strategies at each of these stages in order to minimise your appeal to the psychopath on the hunt.

However, before any of these strategies can work, you have to recognise exactly what you are dealing with when a psychopath comes along. Only then will you be able to combat their menace.

Knowing who and what your enemy is may sound simple. In fact it is anything but, especially with someone as manipulative and completely without conscience as a psychopath. Knowledge is the key to success and the only real chance you have of recognising a psychopath is to arm yourself with knowledge. Put simply, before you can recognise one, you need to know what a psychopath is.

A good knowledge of behavioural characteristics, in addition to understanding how the psychopath thinks, is essential. You need to know how the psychopath targets his victims. It follows that if you know this you can therefore make yourself less of an appeal-ing target. This book for one contains enough information for you to become well acquainted with the psychopath and his mind. Each chapter has been written to help you journey deep into the psychopath's mind and understand what it is that makes such individuals tick.

Having read this far, by now you should be able to tell the difference between the serial killer and the stalker and the motivations for their crimes. You should be able to identify the difference between the office bully and the fraudster. While both may be white-collar psychopaths, they have different reasons for doing what they do.

You should also be able to see that no matter what offence the psychopath commits, be it murder, rape, fraud, or assault, there are a number of fundamental underlying personality traits that bind them all together and which you can identify. You know that all psychopaths are glib and superficial. Likewise you know that they have the gift of the gab and are expert liars and manipulators. As a result of knowing this the next time someone promises you something that sounds too good to be true, you should be able to realise it as being just that and subject it to closer scrutiny before being conned.

Think back to how the psychopath is able to expertly shift from one topic to the next without you initially noticing it. They do this to cover up their lying. So the next time you come across someone who does this, ask yourself why. Is it meant to impress you with their wealth of experience? Or are you in the middle of the contact phase, and is the quick-talking person before you covering his deceit with every sentence?

Of course, merely reading this book is not enough of a weapon in the battle against the psychopath. There are countless numbers of times and situations when you will have met a psychopath and had such a conversation. In fact, there will be many of you who have already been targeted by a psychopath and you probably wouldn't have realised it until it was too late, if at all.

To prevent yourself from becoming the next victim, you have to minimise the psychopath's opportunities for recognising you. Personal security, particularly for women, and particularly at night, should be a major priority for everyone. Don't neglect this issue – remember, if the psychopath can't 'see' you, he can't hurt you either.

Sometimes no matter what you do, it isn't quite enough, for

the psychopath is a determined individual. He will evaluate your fears, doubts and weak points and then exploit them in the manipulation phase.

But the battle is not over. You are not beaten yet, as it is at this phase where you have the greatest amount of control over what is about to happen. Again, though, you are up against a formidable foe – for the con is the psychopath's expertise and it is where his true colours show themselves. The simplest advice we can give anyone at this stage of their involvement with a psychopathic is to think. Think about the veracity of the story being told or the so-called golden opportunity that is being explained. Think about the behavioural clues given away by the suspected psychopath's speech. Think! All the answers are there, staring you in the face. Take a moment to find them. It might save your life.

The eyes of the psychopath are said to be akin to empty black pits, completely without expression or emotion. They appear to see through and beyond you. They are eerie and frightening – the eyes of the devil. We have sat in front of psychopathic offenders and we have spoken to individuals whose behaviour and personality can certainly be said to be psychopathic. In our experience some of them do indeed have dead, menacing eyes that display no emotion or compassion. They look like eyes incapable of shedding tears – empty voids that transmit an evil portent. They are yet another warning sign as to what the person in front of you might be.

It is vital during this phase that you do not deny the potential consequences of what might happen, if you have even the slightest inkling that something might not be right and all is not as it seems. A recent case we came across, involving a serial rapist, illustrated this so-called 'victim denial' perfectly. The rapist would approach his victims carrying a knife and tell them that he only wanted to rob them of their handbag and money. He would then go on to tell them that he didn't want them to scream or chase after him following the robbery and so wanted to tie them up and gag them. The victims, not wanting to believe that they might be raped (which would be realising their deepest fears) as well as robbed, agreed with little resistance to being tied up. Of course, as soon as they were bound and gagged, the women were sexually assaulted. Yet in their minds they doubted what the man was capable of doing and failed to recognise the warning signs in their own minds as to the utter evil of the person standing before them brandishing a knife and wearing a balaclava. This is meant in no way to say that the victims could have prevented the rape from happening and were to blame for what happened to them. Rather it is used as an example of what happens when we fail to confront our fears and understand the diabolical nature of the psychopath.

There is very little you as a victim can do during the so-called kill phase, especially when the offender is a serial killer, rapist or stalker. In the workplace though, there are a number of steps you can take to reduce or eliminate the abuse or trauma you suffer and these will be discussed in the next chapter.

The fraudster, however, can be beaten – even at this late stage. For this type of offender the kill phase comes once the potential victim is asked for money. He or she will try to rush the victim into handing over their cash, saying that there's a pressing deadline that means they have to hand over the money now or the opportunity is lost forever. Think. The fraudster can't get anywhere without your money. Ask yourself what kind of opportunity is it that is lost forever unless you hand over your savings? Does what is on offer sound too good to be true? Are you worried about a particular aspect of the scheme that you're being asked to invest in? If you can answer yes to one of these questions, then do one of two things – either say no, or speak to a trusted accountant or solicitor and get their verdict on the matter.

The final phase is often the hardest to come to terms with. The victim phase, as it is known, is the moment when you realise that you have been the victim of a psychopath. For some people, as we have seen in earlier chapters, this realisation that they are victims is hard to bear.

If you are being bullied at work, or have had money stolen by a smooth-talking conman, then at some stage, you have to admit that the psychopath has got you. The best coping method we can offer is to tell the victim to stop holding out all hope that everything will turn out fine and life will go on as normal. The opposite is much more likely. The key aspect to survival during this phase, is to admit defeat and implement damage limitation strategies. The psychological wellbeing of the victim immediately following this realisation is of paramount importance. Whether you are a victim of a fraud or scam, workplace bully, a rapist, or a stalker, talking about the experience with a trusted friend or psychologist is of the utmost importance. In the same way that the phoenix rises from the ashes, the victim too must learn to grow again, no matter how difficult it might seem immediately following their brush with the devil.

Can this devil change? Can he be rehabilitated? Can he see that what he is doing or has done has caused devastation and is wrong? There are a some psychologists, criminologists and other associated professionals who believe that it is possible to rehabilitate psychopaths. We are not amongst them. We do not believe it is possible to rehabilitate psychopathic offenders. Why do we say this? We believe that their behaviour is a lifelong pattern that is so entrenched in their minds and thought processes that it is simply impossible to attempt to forcefully change it. Therapy, or a prison term, cannot force a fundamental change in someone's personality – and certainly not someone as manipulative and cunning as a psychopath. This is not to say, however, that all criminals in our prisons are psychopaths, nor is it saying these 'non-psychopathic' criminals cannot be rehabilitated.

The development of the psychopath is a gradual process, occurring from very early on in the individual's life. Nature and nurture seemingly conspire against this individual, shaping their perceptions of the world and views in life. Over time, the psychopath comes to see the world as being one where everybody is against them, no one cares for them or loves them unconditionally, and is a place where they feel they have little to no control over their own lives or destinies.

As a child the psychopath sees the world they live in according to a series of distorted perceptions of reality. Over time they come to believe that everything in life is a challenge to their supremacy and control over their own fate. They interpret innocent events in irrational ways, based upon their inferiority complexes. For example, a person cutting them off in traffic is seen as a direct challenge to their existence on earth. Consequently, as we have seen countless numbers of times, the 'offending' driver is taught a brutal and violent lesson by the psychopath in what have become known as road rage incidents. The psychopath then evaluates the success of this behaviour as justifying further acts of violence and control. They figure that because no one has cut them off on the roads since they bashed the last person, what they did must be right and has worked effectively. This is not to say that all instances of 'road rage' are perpetrated by psychopaths. Quite often it is caused by an impulse control problem.

Another example of this is the white-collar psychopath. As we saw earlier, these people bully their colleagues, quite often their subordinates, which results in two forms of success. Firstly, they are psychologically rewarded because they can see very clearly the degree of control and domination they are able to exert over the victims. Secondly, they are rewarded in society by the fact that they are paid considerable salaries and bonuses for apparent increases in productivity. In addition, they are often promoted because of their high achievement rates.

It pays to remember that these types of people evaluate what they do in terms of how satisfied it makes them. Conscience does not come into it at all. There is no remorse or guilt. They do not care if other people suffer, particularly the weak minnows below them at their place of work. This personality and approach to life has taken years to develop and every day is reinforced by a deluded belief system. There is only one person who can change this and without exception, that person, the psychopath, doesn't want to change.

This is another reason why all psychopaths cannot be 'cured'. Many white-collar psychopaths are never caught. That is why they are so frightening – they are all around us and we often don't know who they are until it's too late. Therefore if they are not caught, the white-collar psychopath will move from job to job continuing his behaviour wherever he or she is employed. Likewise, there are a number of active serial killers currently on the loose and destined never to be caught simply because they are too intelligent and they know the system inside out. They are far too good at what they do, and knowing this as they undoubtedly do, they see no reason for giving up their criminal behaviour. The crimes work for them. They are fulfilled. Why change?

So, if the ones that aren't caught can't be changed, what about those psychopaths who have been caught and convicted and are currently in jails around the country?

Prisons serve three functions. They are there to punish offenders for their actions; to attempt to rehabilitate or reform the individual; and to protect society from the individual until such time as the offender is reformed. We will concentrate on the issues of rehabilitation and the protection of society – a discussion on the effectiveness of punishment as an ethical concept is not what this book is intended for.

It is impossible, in our opinion, to even begin to attempt to change the psychological make-up of psychopaths to enable them to have true respect and compassion for their fellow man. The psychopath doesn't care about anyone other than himself. The psychopath doesn't care about society.

The very nature of the psychopath's mind makes this so. These people have lived with their beliefs and psychology for many years. This ensures that when it comes to therapy, psychopaths are the most resistant clients there are. Everything that is said to them is simply negated in their heads as being inappropriate. All of their behaviour and each of their actions are evaluated from their point of view and their point of view only. This means that no matter what offence they have committed, be it the vicious murder of a woman or the defrauding of an elderly couple, they can psychologically avoid comprehending what it is they have done.

We have said, perhaps too many times, that psychopaths have no conscience and lack emotion. These instincts cannot be replicated. We do not know how to create emotions and a conscience and then transplant them into the mind of a psychopath. There is no adequate framework at present to effectively devise therapies for the treatment of antisocial personality disorders.

At many of our lectures we are asked why this is the case. In short, therapy relies to a large extent on the client's voluntary participation, self-reporting and willingness to change. Does this sound like something a convicted psychopath would be interested in? Do you think that a lying, cheating and manipulating individual like the offenders we have described could be trusted to participate in therapy when it relies on all of the above? We know that the psychopath does not want treatment.

They don't want to change. As a result everything the therapist says is dismissed and resisted. Don't be fooled by the deranged killer who says he has changed or found God. The psychopath has a vested interest in appearing rehabilitated because it helps them secure parole. If they do attend therapy sessions, they will use all of their charm and manipulative powers to convince those in authority that they have changed for the better. They will do and say whatever they can to get out of prison and back on the street where they can once again return to doing what it is that makes them feel alive.

The issue of rehabilitation becomes ever more cloudy when you associate it with the serial killer or rapist. Sex is thrown into the equation and when combined with power and control, it is nigh on impossible to redirect these motivators and channel them into something more normal.

The serial killer or rapist evolves once their latent aggression and low self-esteem finds an outlet in the form of rape or murder. These feelings are deep and well entrenched. They are impossible to shift. They are a lost cause.

Chemical or physical castration has been cited as a possible method of rehabilitation for the rapist or paedophile, but once again we believe that this is a non-starter. Rape, sexual homicide and paedophilia are not solely about sex – they are tools for gaining power and control as a means to compensate for low self-esteem. In fact many serial killers are impotent at the time of their crimes, as was the case with John Wayne Glover, the Granny Killer.

An angry psychopathic offender, who has a problem with society for a start, is not going to feel much better when he is castrated. Yes, he may have raped and killed a young girl. Yes, he may deserve whatever it is he has coming to him. But in doing this, would we not be creating an even angrier individual? If this man was released, wouldn't he feel the need to take this anger out on somebody, somewhere, meaning yet another innocent person would end up the victim of a monster bent on revenge?

So what do we do with these people, these devils who can't be rehabilitated? Do we lock them up forever and throw away the key in order to protect society? Do we release them and give them another chance, as happens too many times to mention? Do we execute them so that they can pose no further danger or expense to society? Or do we study them in prison and try to come up with ways in which they can be rehabilitated?

Each one of us has our own view as to what should be done with convicted psychopaths. While we won't use this forum to express our personal views, we will go on record as saying that we find it totally unacceptable that some of these individuals who cannot and will not be rehabilitated are regularly released from prison to re-offend time and time again.

No doubt there will be some people out there who disagree with us and say that psychopathy will be eliminated. We would say that they are correct, just as in theory people who say it is possible to land a manned spacecraft on Pluto are correct. Unfortunately, we are not advanced enough as yet, and we do not have the systems in place, to land a manned vessel on the surface of Pluto, although we might be able to do so in another 100 years. Likewise, we are not able at present to defeat psychopathy. The time might well come when we are able. But until then, these dangerous individuals should be kept well away from society and we must become wiser to their threat.

CHAPTER 11

Coping with the Devil

Many people are shocked when we tell them that psychopaths are found in the majority of workplaces. It is a terrifying statement and one that we do not make lightly. It is a frightening thought that potentially in any top corporation – as well as in lesser-known firms – there will be at least one psychopath working there full-time.

He or she will be hidden from senior management by virtue of their superior manipulative abilities and sheer intelligence. This white-collar psychopath will be hard to flush out, and even harder to contain if they are allowed to flourish. They will disrupt the flow of work, intimidate their fellow workers and destroy all semblance of order. How can we stop them?

On many occasions we have been called into a company to help identify possible psychopathic threats. On arriving at the company, the first question we are always asked is how exactly we will be able to identify these chameleons when they are well adept at hiding behind false facades and so supremely skilful at playing the system and invariably winning. In this final chapter, we will provide you with some answers as to how we unmask the devil. We will take you with us as we hunt the hunter.

Our experience has shown that there are two types of psychopathic individual usually encountered in the workplace. The first type, and always the most physically dangerous, is the criminal psychopath.

This individual has a job for no other reason but to provide him with the means to survive. It provides him with a sense of security and some money, and career advancement is definitely not the primary focus in this person's life. For this reason we would expect to find that this individual is likely to have moved from one job to the next in low- to medium-skilled professions. Without fail, they will have a problem with authority, breaking rules, intimidating and possibly even assaulting co-workers wherever they might be. Like all psychopaths these men – and this type of white-collar psychopath is almost always a male – display no sense of responsibility with regards to their jobs, and see it merely as a vehicle to earn money and appear legitimate in order to conceal their criminal behaviour, which is the real purpose of their lives.

We find other criminal white-collar psychopaths in middle- to upper-level management positions – a result of their focus on their career and their obsession with needing to appear legitimate within society to cover for their other illicit activities. Often these individuals are very intelligent and methodical. They are extremely effective at what they do, and usually stay with their chosen organisation for a prolonged period of time. It is commonly as a result of this long service that they are promoted, as opposed to their outstanding natural abilities within their profession.

Victims are found within these psychopath's spheres of influence – in other words, where they work. It's often hard to believe that there are people we work with every day who are predators, using their time at the workplace to actively seek a new victim. It's hard to believe, but unfortunately it's true. It's highly unlikely, unless you knew exactly what you were looking for, that you would be able to recognise these individuals for what they are. These people are skilful in deceit and give daily performances worthy of Academy Awards. They emit an air of normality. On the surface they look, act and talk like every one else. Yet on the inside they are raging tempests barely able to contain themselves.

In this chapter we will focus on the psychological procedures we adopt when trying to capture these individuals before they can cause any further carnage. We say 'before they can cause any further carnage' because unfortunately before we can even begin to look at identifying the criminal psychopath, there has to be a victim, or victims. Once we have a victim, we can use criminal investigative analysis or criminal psychological profiling as an aid to any investigation aimed at apprehending a criminal psychopath.

Criminal profiling is undertaken for the main part on cases that involve murder or a series of rapes or sexual assaults. A vital parameter of profiling is the narrowing down of the number of potential suspects who *could* have committed the crime. The profile also helps to highlight the character type and psychological make-up of the psychopathic killer or rapist.

In their 1995 book, *Practical Aspects of Rape Investigation* (2nd edn) former FBI special agent Roy Hazelwood and Ann Burgess, a professor of psychiatric nursing and rape trauma specialist, highlight precisely what type of investigations can be helped by employing profiling techniques:

'While virtually any crime showing mental, emotional, or personality aberration can be analysed for profiling purposes, certain crimes are particularly appropriate for the process. These crimes include a series of rapes, lust murder (mutilation or displacement of the sexual areas of the body), serial murders, child molesting, ritualistic crimes, threat communications, violence in the workplace, and serial arson.'

All of these offences have been investigated in this book. Without exception, they are offences that are committed by psychopaths.

Criminal profiling as a concept can be traced back to the earliest principles of criminology. It is now an accepted theory that whenever a crime is committed, an exchange takes place between the criminal and the crime scene. In a nutshell the criminal always leaves a part of himself at the scene of the crime – be it a fingerprint, his DNA, semen, or a psychological signature or behavioural shadow – and always takes some of the crime scene away with him. Profiling is the art of interpreting what is left behind and then developing an understanding of who has done the crime through looking at that offender's unique 'work'.

The principles underpinning profiling have been recognised in literature since Edgar Allen Poe's *Murders in the Rue Morgue*, and Arthur Conan Doyle's character, Sherlock Holmes, who used to make inferences about an offender's personality from evidence found at the scene of the crime. In the non-fiction world, the pioneer of criminal personality profiling was an American psychiatrist, Dr James Brussel. In 1956, Brussel was approached by the New York City Police Department to compile a psychological profile of the Mad Bomber of New York.

After studying crime scene photographs and analysing letters the Mad Bomber had written taunting police, Brussel came up with a profile of the offender. It proved to be uncannily accurate. He said the offender would be a white male, unmarried, Eastern European immigrant who was a Roman Catholic and living in Connecticut. He went on to say that when the offender was arrested he would be wearing a double-breasted suit that would be fully buttoned.

Within days of the profile being handed over, a suspect was arrested. His name was George Metesky and he fit the profile like a glove. He was an immigrant, a Roman Catholic, he lived in Connecticut, and he was unmarried. When police apprehended him, Metesky was wearing a double-breasted suit – fully buttoned.

Brussel's achievement was seen as nothing short of amazing. Law enforcement officials, the media, and the general public, could not comprehend how it was possible for the psychiatrist to know such intimate details about a complete stranger. Brussel stated that he was simply working backwards to what he was used to. In his daily work, he was used to seeing a person first and then learning about their behaviour later. In the case of the Mad Bomber, he already had the behaviour – he simply needed to figure out the personality of the offender. Criminal profiling was born.

The FBI rapidly developed a keen interest in the art of profiling following Brussel's success. A number of agents met with Brussel and learnt as much as they could about uncovering the psychology of an offender. By the late 1970s, Special Agents Robert Ressler and John Douglas were compiling the first thorough research on the motives and behavioural patterns of sexual homicide offenders. The work, which was later published under the title *Sexual Homicide: Patterns and Motives*, involved the agents interviewing 36 convicted sexual homicide offenders. They gained a unique insight into the minds of these depraved killers. Ressler and Douglas learnt how serial killers such as Ted Bundy and John Wayne Gacy thought, and what compelled them to embark on their killing sprees. Criminal profiling is now used as an investigative tool around the world, and is well established in the UK.

So what does profiling involve and how is a profile developed? How can we look inside the devil's mind? Essentially profiling is most effective for unusual crimes in which a psychological part of the offender remains at the scene. In general profiling would not be too useful in terms of developing a likely suspect for a run-of-the-mill domestic burglary. It could identify a likely type of offender, but the number of people who would fit this type would be so large as to render the profile ineffective. However, if some unusual behaviour has been exhibited at the burglary – for example the offender has masturbated into a victim's underwear drawer – profiling would be far more effective. In this case, it is clear that we are not dealing with an everyday house burglar. Here, we are dealing with a completely different type of offender who is much less common.

A thorough understanding of the psychology of the offender can be a particularly valuable tool in the investigation of predatory crimes, such as sexual homicide and sexual assault. For this reason in recent years offender profiling has become a more accepted tool in the arsenal employed by police in serious criminal investigations.

While no single predator is exactly the same, common patterns of offender behaviour and personality traits have been observed. These patterns, or typologies, as they are referred to, can tell you a great deal about an offender.

A profiler with enough clinical and forensic experience can actually make predictions about what sort of person the offender is likely to be, where they can be found, and how they will behave in the future. Information such as demographic characteristics (age, marital status, occupation, residence, type of vehicle owned), personality characteristics, criminal history, physical characteristics, pre- and post-offence behaviour, as well as investigation recommendations, can all be provided once an understanding of the offender's personality has been reached.

To prepare a profile, three things must be done. Firstly the would-be profiler must determine from the victim (if the victim is alive of course) what type of behaviour was exhibited by the offender during the attack. Secondly, the profiler must analyse that behaviour in an attempt to determine the offender's motivation. Finally, he or she must then highlight the set of characteristics and personality traits they believe a person would have to have for them to commit such an offence in a similar manner.

Paul Britton, author of *The Jigsaw Man,* and one of Britain's leading profilers, says that there are four essential questions that must be asked by a profiler when compiling a profile – what happened, how, to whom, and why. Without answers to these questions, he says, there will be no profile and inevitably no suspect – there will be no answer to the fifth and most important question, who.

To learn about the offender we have to think like the offender, and that is what profiling allows us to do. By finding out the what, how, to whom, and why, we begin to get a clear picture of the driving forces that propel the offender to commit what is without exception a terrible act.

A large amount of information needs to be collated before a profile can be compiled and work. The first essential ingredients in any profile are what are termed the profiling inputs. These include such factors as crime scene photographs, the physical evidence, the position of the body and the presence or absence of any weapons at the crime scene. Forensic information regarding the cause of death, patterns of wounds observed on the body, any pre- or post-mortem sex acts, as well as the autopsy and laboratory reports are also invaluable.

All of this information assists in determining what has actually happened and how it has occurred. This in turn allows the profiler to formulate a composite picture of the sequence of events. It is the spinal column of the profile. This information also tells us to a limited extent what went on between the offender and the victim. The offender of course already knows all of this. To get into his mind we too, as profilers, have to know this. We need to know what exactly the psychopath is getting out of the crime and when we know this, we know what motivates him.

What is even more important to know is what was physically done to the victim. The psychological factors underlying each and every single one of these acts helps us in the eventual identification of the offender.

Looking at the area where the crime was committed also helps in providing a workable profile to the relevant investigative bodies. We need to know whether the area has a particularly high or low crime rate, what time the crime occurred, who reported the crime and the socio-economic status of the crime area. Each of these factors allows the profiler to place himself at the scene before the crime was committed. He sees the scene as the offender did and gradually with each and every piece of additional information he delves further into the offender's mind.

This is a critical aspect of any profile. We need to learn what the offender knows about the crime scene and the area surrounding it. We need to know whether the location the body was found at or where the offence actually took place holds some sort of psychological significance for the offender. To him, invariably, it is more than just a place. It is a place with a special meaning and symbolism all of its own. It signifies the place where the offender was able, for a moment, to gain complete power and control over another human being. It is a site at which they have performed one of their most personal rituals.

While we now know what happened to the victim and where

this offence occurred we still do not have enough information for an accurate profile. We need to know as much as we can about the behavioural interactions that occurred as part of the offence. This is yet another way in which we can view the crime from the offender's perspective, and understand what he was thinking at the time of the crime.

The offence itself is an interaction between two people – the offender and the victim. In order to get a full picture of what has happened we must also look at the crime from the victim's point of view. The victim tells us a lot about the offender. Who is the victim? Where do they live? Where do they work? What were they doing in the area at the time of the attack? Where had they been? What is their family life like? Who do they live with? Who are their friends? What were the victim's hobbies, or interests? What kind of person were they?

There is something about the victim that appeals to the killer. Analysing the answers to these questions could help us pinpoint that specific factor. It helps us to understand the role fantasy played in the offence. If we can figure out the fantasy we can get a much clearer picture of the psychology of the offender. Not only this, but the fantasy element may be repeated in each crime the offender commits. It will become part of his methodology, his signature if you like.

It is at this moment, that we have the three pieces of the puzzle that we need to form a workable and accurate profile. Now we have to evaluate what has actually occurred. In order to do this, it is necessary to recreate or imagine the crime in all its brutality from the perspective of the two people involved. We see the crime through two sets of eyes – the victim's and the offender's. Each person's behaviour will influence the overall outcome of the crime. We evaluate the risk level of the victim. From this we can evaluate the risk for the offender in executing his crime. Obviously, a prostitute walking the streets at two in the morning has a higher risk than a secretary working at an office in the middle of the day. The lower the risk level, the more intelligent the offender. He also probably has a good level of previous criminal experience, which would have a direct bearing on his age.

We need to visualise the interaction between the two people. Did the offender become more aroused during the rape/murder? Did the offender perform sexual acts at the crime scene, and if they did, were they performed pre- or post-mortem? How did the offender select the victim and how was the victim initially controlled? What sequence of acts were performed and in what order? Did the offender arrive at the scene prepared for the crime? Has the offender removed any items of the victim's property from the scene or taken any other souvenirs? What does all of this tell us of his motivation?

We then look at the injuries suffered by the victim at the hands of the killer, as these tell us how experienced the offender is in dealing with death. Was the victim stabbed or strangled? Was the victim dismembered? When contemplating mutilation and dismemberment, as with everything in life, practice makes perfect. Certain types of serial killer become highly efficient in disposing of their victim's bodies. The increase in mutilation and the manner in which a victim is dismembered helps us to learn the level of offender progression. In addition, if cannibalism is present it helps us to narrow down our range of potential suspects still further.

These are just some of the many questions we must ask in attempting to create a profile of the psychopathic offender. From the answers we gather, we can then come to a conclusion about the motivation or driving forces for the offender. We can enter his mind. We can then begin to make predictions about who he is and how he is likely to behave.

Establishing the offender's motivation allows us to start looking for a likely suspect. However, profiling is more than just about providing a simple sketch of a possible offender. It also helps provide investigation strategies for the relevant police and law enforcement bodies that will be involved on the case. Because the profiler understands the motivation of the offender, he also has a good grasp on how that offender will behave before, during, and after his next crime, if he is not caught beforehand.

The impact of the profile does not end once a suspect is captured. It also helps provide investigators with an understanding of how the offender thinks, and highlights the most appropriate methods that could be used to increase the chances of a confession being made when the suspect is interviewed. How detectives speak to the offender is a matter of grave importance.

For some types of serial killer, talking about the murders they have committed is a deeply personal thing. They have spent all of their lives revealing absolutely nothing to anyone about their fantasies or beliefs. Simply sitting down in front of them and asking them to tell you everything about their crimes is unlikely to produce much of a response. They will tell you nothing, and if they do confess to anything, it is unlikely to be the truth. To have them reveal their deepest and darkest thoughts – their true motivations and fantasies – involves a logical progression.

The other type of workplace psychopath we have encountered in our work is one who does not engage in physically destructive or criminal behaviour. Instead, these individuals embark on the trail of psychological destruction of their co-workers, spouses and neighbours – in short whomever they can readily destroy.

There are a number of important factors to consider when dealing with this type of white-collar psychopath. Firstly, they do provide higher levels of productivity. However, this is often achieved through the use of psychological abuse and terror tactics directed toward their staff. Increased levels of productivity may also be achieved because these individuals are extremely good manipulators who promise the world but fail to deliver.

Not surprisingly, considering his impact on the bottom line, this type of psychopath is often viewed by the senior management of the firm as a being a valuable employee. The suspect person regularly achieves high levels of productivity from their subordinates through the use of terror or bully tactics. This behaviour goes unnoticed. In the process, the psychopath makes money for the business. For some companies that is all that matters, generating revenue is the be all and end all. In turn these destructive men and women are rewarded for their behaviour with promotions, high wages, stock ownership schemes and hefty bonuses. How they manage to achieve this is a testament to their intelligence.

Usually they make promises to customers or clients that they cannot keep. Over time these false promises undermine them and the world they build around themselves begins to crumble. But before any of this can happen, the psychopath needs to make friends with the people in charge – if he can become one of the boys, so to speak, then when things go wrong, he can escape the blame.

In the short term everything goes well for the psychopath. Profits are made and the business performs consistently well. The psychopath undermines the senior management's perception and belief in staff. He highlights to his bosses potential 'troublemakers' within the office. These troublemakers are usually the psychopath's subordinate staff and are innocent victims of the psychopath's twisted mind. Staff turnover rates are therefore exceptionally high. One company we dealt with in Sydney had a staff turnover rate of 85 per cent in just six months – all because of one man, who was so good at his job that he was personally responsible for over half of the company's business.

So how does someone like this manage to position themself within a company and make themselves so indispensable within it that other long-term employees are no longer believed by senior management as being effective?

The strategy we have seen to make this happen is quite simple, but very effective, as all the best strategies are. The psychopath will start his employment with the company at the middle level of management, depending, of course, upon their experience and ability to manipulate their interviewers. Charming, glib, superficial and possessing excellent verbal skills, they will say and do all the right things to make the job their own. Once in the job, they will very quickly evaluate their co-workers and assess their individual wants and needs. Then they will begin their campaign of hate.

Very quickly they will become friendly with each of the people they work with. This will happen over a short space of time, and in some cases can happen in less than a couple of weeks. They will then set about convincing this group of people that they are a vital component of it. To do this effectively, they will seek out the weakest link and commence a period of character assassination and humiliation towards that person. Within weeks, they will have fellow workers on their side and eventually they will be seen as the leader of this group, which is united against a perceived common enemy, namely the weak co-worker.

This unity with the group ensures the psychopath is liked and respected by his fellow workers. They come to rely upon him. Pretty soon they will come to fear him, as they begin to realise that what has happened to their colleague could well happen to them in the future. Interestingly, Adolf Hitler was particularly adept at this. The German dictator utilised a similar divide and conquer strategy, which he called *führerprinzip* (the Leadership Principle). He managed to manipulate and dominate a Cabinet and nation by playing people off against one another and instilling a sense of fear in even his closest of colleagues. The white-collar psychopath in the office blocks of today, does exactly the same thing, except on a smaller scale.

As a result of his actions, there is now a disruption to the harmony and culture within the workplace. At this moment, the psychopath will turn himself into a saviour – at least in the senior management's eyes. Basically, he will resolve the conflict he himself has started. He will do this by either encouraging the innocent victim to leave or through welcoming him or her back into the fold after 'counselling' them as to their inefficiencies.

The resolution of the crisis is witnessed by the company's grateful senior management, and suddenly the psychopath's star begins to rise. As he gains increasing contact with the senior management, and they gain more confidence in him, he will voice complaints about the attributes and abilities of his fellow workers – colleagues who believe the psychopath is their friend. All along, the psychopath will trust no one. Any person who gets in his or her way will have their reputation destroyed, or will be subjected to unbearable psychological abuse. In short, this white-collar psychopath will do all he or she can to get rid of the person they see as a threat.

With the psychopath's star now on a higher level, promotion quickly follows. He or she is seen as being an essential asset to the business – a key component of the company's success and ironically, its harmony. The rewards come thick and fast.

Throughout all of this the psychopath remains in contact with a more senior manager than their own. There is a simple and logical reason for this – the psychopath wants his manager's job and is destroying the reputation and character of his boss to the man higher up. At the same time, the psychopath acts as if his or her boss is their best friend. They do this to ensure that when the deception becomes apparent, it is a complete surprise and no resistance is offered. Their boss's job becomes their own.

With the psychopath as their new manager, former colleagues are put firmly in their place. They become tools for the psychopath to use to impress his senior managers. They also help sate the offender's desire for power and control over someone. Bitter and confused, but unable to do anything about it, the staff invariably clear away their desks and at short notice leave their jobs.

As we would expect this destructive behaviour continues. The office psychopath abuses whoever remains beneath them to such an extent that productivity levels are boosted. In return, the psychopath is once again rewarded for his or her work. The cycle continues. Abuse and reward. Abuse and reward.

The important factor to consider when looking at this common strategy is that it achieves a lot more than simply a promotion and fatter bank balance for the psychopath. It actually results in them being seen as a crucial facet of the company's culture. They are known by everyone – hated by those below them who have been used, but seen as valuable by those above them. Upper management often refuses to believe anything negative that is said about the psychopath as they have been completely taken in by an expert and skilful manipulator. Without fail these experienced senior managers, will defend the reputation of a psychopath at all costs. Men and women who are paid hundreds of thousands of pounds each year to head up some of the UK's largest companies fail to see that they are being conned by someone they think they know and believe they trust.

How does this happen? How does a psychopath manage to psychologically destroy his work colleagues and what can you do to protect yourself against them?

The psychopath derives a high degree of personal pleasure in destroying the people closest to him. As you are aware by now, psychopaths everywhere target the weakest members of society. This is no different in the white-collar world.

The isolation of their victim is accomplished through either fear or manipulation. Once isolated the psychopath will begin to break the victim down, systematically forcing increased amounts of stress and pressure upon them, all the while targeting psychological weak points. Precisely what these weak points are will depend to a large extent on the victim. It may be an issue of self-esteem, particularly with regard to the way the victim looks or acts. Verbal and sexual harassment, combined with the bullying of the victim, will be carried out simultaneously. Whatever is needed to break down the victim will be done. Over a prolonged period of time the isolated individual becomes increasingly stressed. Their ability to mentally resist the psychopath decreases until eventually they are unable to cope with even the smallest of issues or tasks at their workplace.

When this point is reached, the psychopath moves up a gear in more ways than one. Firstly he will go to the senior management of the company and inform them of his supposedly useless subordinate and recommend that they be fired. He will get his way, as the senior managers will have no idea that the reason for the person's dramatic decline in achievement is the systematic campaign of personal destruction put in place by the psychopath.

Secondly, now sensing that he is invincible, he will expand his exploitation of staff – in some instances this might be achieved by forcing junior female members to feel obligated to have sex with him. In one case that we have dealt with, a white-collar psychopath had sexual relations with the entire junior female staff in his department – all 20 of them. When questioned about what went on, all the victims of this man said they felt obliged to have sex with him because he said that if they didn't they would lose their jobs.

Two critical components are needed if a solution to the problem of white-collar psychopaths of the type we have just described is to be found – the company's response to the problem, and the individual's response. For any solution to work, both components must be implemented simultaneously.

In terms of the employee response to the psychopath, the most important factor is to ensure that no one is ever isolated. The psychopath isolates their victim from everybody prior to moving in for the kill. If they are unable to single out any one person, it will prove much more difficult for their strategy to work. If a unified body of people confronts the psychopath each time they attempt to victimise an individual they will eventually become frustrated with the situation, and realise that there have to be easier avenues to satisfy their need for power and control. In short, they will move on.

To deal effectively with a psychopath at the office, every employee needs to have a high level of self-esteem. The happier each person is with themselves and their place in society, the less likely they are to become a victim. If however, you do find yourself the unwitting target of a psychopath, it is vital that you find someone to talk to about the experience. If you fail to do this, you will very quickly lose your sense of self-esteem and find that you are easy picking for the psychopath. Once this happens, you will be unlikely to stop the attack.

It helps greatly if a potential victim has some understanding of the psychology behind the psychopath. This enables them to realise that what is happening is not their fault, while at the same time allows them to see that they are being preyed upon by an abnormal person who is not restrained by normal human emotions. It lets them realise that they are pawns in one person's very sick game.

Do not feel guilt about being a victim. We cannot emphasise too strongly the importance of talking to someone you trust about what is happening. Merely talking about the situation may not stop it, but it will reinforce in your mind that the problem is not of your making and is in no way your fault. It will make you understand that you are not guilty for what is happening – you have done nothing wrong.

Quite often victims tell us that at the time of the campaign against them, they felt totally alone and as if they had no support whatsoever. If you are currently a victim of a white-collar psychopath, then we recommend that you contact someone immediately with regards to your situation.

Another important consideration in terms of how best to deal with white-collar psychopaths and what action to take, is to evaluate the situation from a rational rather than emotional viewpoint. Sometimes the best policy to adopt in order to rid yourself of the psychopath's attention is to cut your losses and leave your place of work. This may not sound fair. It isn't. But all too often it is the only way to avoid the stress and mental anguish that is piled upon you by the psychopath. Leaving your job and looking for a new position may sound like a hard choice to make – but at the end of the day, clearing your desk and moving out could prevent you suffering a nervous breakdown in the future.

Don't feel that you have lost because of this. You haven't. For one thing, you have kept your sanity and your health. You have also kept your dignity and proved your courage in making what is one of life's most difficult decisions.

From the corporate viewpoint the first question any company should ask itself if it believes a psychopath exists within the structure is this: what benefit does the psychopath bring? On initial inspection, it may appear that the individual is helping to increase productivity, making more sales, or boosting the company's profitability. But look a little closer, get beneath the facade, and you will undoubtedly find something infinitely more worrying.

It's a fairly safe bet that the psychopath's unpleasant manner towards his or her staff is actually resulting in poorer service levels, lower customer satisfaction levels, and customer and staff retention problems. A demoralised team of staff is something you don't want if your aim is to run a profitable and competitive business in what is an increasingly service-driven economy. Try to find out how your suspected psychopath conducts their business. To make a sale, do they offer customers false promises that your company cannot possibly meet? Find out how many dissatisfied customers there are out there – there will be a lot and your reputation may well be tarnished as a result.

Another crucial factor corporations need to ask themselves regards the cost of hiring and training staff. A high staff turnover rate in a company is a sure sign that a psychopath exists within the network. How much does this cost the company? Likewise, high levels of sick leave and occupational health and safety claims could also be pointers to the possibility of the existence of a white-collar psychopath.

Any reduction in the impact of the psychopath on the company depends on what action is taken and what net result is desired. Most companies get stuck on two choices. On the one hand they feel they should terminate the psychopath's contract, while on the other, some companies opt to keep the psychopath and attempt to minimise the potential for damage.

Which conclusion is reached is controlled by the personality of the psychopath – some are able to be channelled towards so-called 'good' activities, while for others it is far more economical and safe to lose them from the company altogether.

Regardless of what action is taken, the initial step must be a general acceptance by senior level management that there is a problem. A consultant should be hired to help assess the degree of the problem and whether the individual concerned may be labelled as being psychopathic or not. This consultant would educate senior management about psychopathy in addition to assessing the options available for the particular case.

The recognition of a psychopath or even a difficult employee is often the most neglected area in business. On many occasions senior management do not listen to their lower level staff. In addition, they see a consultant as an unnecessary expense and the situation remains largely ignored and is allowed to fester. They fail to see that dealing with this problem is part of the business process. More importantly it is an obligation of the employer to look after the welfare of its staff and to ensure that they are safe in their place of work. Ignoring these facts could prove to be a very costly and wrong decision in the long term. Attending a professional lecture on this area is essential in assessing whether a problem exists or not.

For a company that decides it wants to retain the services of the psychopathic individual, a specific set of interventions is required. Initially, the other staff need to be educated about psychopathy as a disorder, so that they can protect themselves and recognise when an individual is trying to manipulate them.

Basically the staff need to learn how the psychopath operates so they can respond before any damage is done. Team building is an essential element in defeating the psychopath. You may recall that the white-collar psychopath almost without fail targets individuals. If this person sees that they are up against a team, then the psychopath will move on, looking for more suitable and easier victims.

Once a cohesive team unit has been built another intervention strategy can be utilised to minimise still further the impact of the psychopath. We know that the psychopath is only interested in undertaking jobs or tasks that hold a benefit for themselves. With no individual to prey upon because of the efficacy of the team approach, the psychopath can be presented with an offer that for them is too good to refuse and appeals to their massive egos and ingrained narcissism. Basically, they are given a special task or job, which has the potential of huge performance linked bonuses.

The task varies depending upon the industry involved. An example we have come across involved an individual in a corporation who was given the task of detecting fraudulent financial claims – with each one detected being linked to a performance bonus. This task utilised the individual's talent for recognising the scam. He would have felt fantastic about the power he had over the people he was investigating, and the company reported a significant increase in the number of fraudulent cases detected. It was a winning solution to an otherwise hopeless situation.

If, on the other hand, the psychopath is judged to be too costly in terms of human capital, a strategy must be implemented to ensure their departure is as non-eventful as possible. Once again a thorough understanding of the psychopath is critical. The individual must be presented with a perceived benefit that they simply cannot refuse. Remember these people always do whatever it takes to please themselves. No loyalty to the company or anyone else exists, so they will quickly evaluate or sometimes simply take up a favourable looking opportunity whenever it is presented.

If this option is taken, then the company must minimise the risk of possible sabotage or extortion from the psychopath once he has departed. The psychopath must be given the impression that he or she has won – they must be made to feel they have taken advantage of the company and hoodwinked its directors to have been given the chance of the amazing opportunity that is sitting in front of them. What is this opportunity? Once again, it depends on the individual concerned.

There are millions of psychopaths out there, we know this for certain. They all have the potential to cause mayhem and destruction. They all have a common ability of being able to wreck lives.

We can fight back, but for the moment we do not have enough weapons in our arsenal to be able to defeat them completely. More research needs to be done if we are ever to uncover what it is that makes these people the monsters they are.

Without this research we are all under threat. Our society is in danger of collapse. We can beat them, if we find out what makes them tick. Only then will we be able to prevent more of us from becoming victims. Only then will we protect ourselves from being touched by the devil.

Note from John Clarke

When I started lecturing on criminal psychology and serial killers to police officers and psychology students, I realised very quickly that these two groups not only displayed a professional interest in how the psychopath thinks, but they were fascinated on a personal level as well. Both groups were completely engrossed in the picture of the psychopath I was presenting, attempting to find the answers to two questions: How different are they from us, and what can we do to prevent them from harming us? At first I thought this fascination was unique to those people who had chosen in some way to deal professionally with either criminality or psychology. Then I started allowing a few members of the general public into lectures, and the number of people wanting to attend continued to grow beyond anything I had thought possible. At one point I found myself unable to keep up with the media requests for interviews about serial killers, and unable to deal with the number of people wanting to attend a lecture. It was at this point that I discovered people's fascination with psychopathy is more fundamental than simply a professional interest. Instead, it seems to be a topic that interests a wide spectrum of people. The questions everyone wants answered, however, remain the same: How are they so different from us, are they born or made this way, and how can we protect ourselves from these human predators?

Psychopaths has attempted to explore an incredibly complex subject through examining psychopathy in its major forms – from the serial killer through to the workplace psychopath. An excellent model that I have found useful in lectures that can be applied to help us in our understanding of the formation and cognitive processes of the psychopath is 'chaos' theory. Chaos theory argues that events which occur in nature are characterised by an infinite number of possibilities. However, from these many complex possibilities, systematic patterns can be found. These patterns of life experience are crucial for us to understand because they contain information about why we do the things we do.

What are the patterns or events common to these psychopaths' lives? We have seen psychopaths have a number of physiological abnormalities present from birth (not that we can ever know whether they were present at birth or developed later on, to test for this would be highly unethical). I would argue these physical abnormalities are the building blocks upon which a unique social environment shapes the individual over a period of time into a psychopath. We have seen that for psychopaths there is generally a low level of self-esteem as a result of negative childhood or adolescent experiences. The psychopath somehow develops a response of satiating this need to feel in control of themselves through dominating and controlling those around them. They consistently view the world around them as a hostile place in which only the fittest survive. It is the pattern of their developmental and adult life experiences that shapes how they satisfy their needs for power and control. Some turn to killing people, some to rape, some to psychologically destroying people they work with. Each of these different forms of predator thinks fundamentally the same, though the behavioural expression of their thoughts is very different.

I think the most disturbing aspect of psychopathy for me, is the fact these individuals are completely unaware, and probably will never have insight into the fact that the only way they can ever hope to feel control within themselves is through actually dealing with their own issues as opposed to displacing their aggression and sense of inadequacy onto other people.

Hopefully this brings you a little closer to answering the first question raised by people, how do these people turn out to be so different from ourselves.

In response to how we can prevent these predators from harming us, there are different preventative methods that have been developed. Victim responses also need to be looked at to help in understanding how to minimise the potential danger of the psychopathic individual. Each of these areas is critical in terms of both understanding the true impact of the psychopath and attempting to minimise this impact. The psychopath destroys the lives of their victims in so many ways, but the most amazing thing I have seen as a result of the psychopath's behaviour is the path of personal and spiritual growth they force their victims to embark upon. For the victim, their life is changed forever, but positive growth is still possible. Time and support play massive roles in this. I never cease to be amazed at the resilience of the human spirit. I like to compare the victims I deal with to the phoenix rising from the ashes, stronger and more powerful than it ever was before. This book is really a tribute to the victims of psychopaths, for it is these people who truly inspire courage and hope and faith in the future. It is the victims I deal with who encourage me to continue to educate people in an attempt to minimise the impact of the psychopath on future potential victims. Through their response to their suffering and pain, they not only grow themselves but they also inspire other people such as myself to greater things.

Psychopaths provides a glimpse into the world of specific psychopaths and their victims. Unfortunately there are as many types of psychopathic expression of behaviour again as have been recounted here. There are the paedophiles, the arsonists, and the children who kill their classmates, the organised criminals, the hit men, drug dealers and terrorists. The list goes on, and for each type the fundamental pattern of development is similar.

Unfortunately, there are enough other forms of psychopath to write a book entirely different but just as large as this one. Even for the types of psychopath described here, there is so much information and so many variations that a book could be written on each. This is the extent of the problem not only in Great Britain, but the rest of the Western world face. We do not even know the extent of psychopathy in second and third world nations.

It is for this reason that I continue to talk about serial murder, rape, workplace psychopaths and all of the other unpleasant manifestations of psychopathic behaviour. I believe it is imperative that not only should I educate law enforcement personnel in the hope that more of these individuals may be apprehended, but that I also provide the same level of knowledge to the general public so that you have the best possible chance of recognising and understanding how the psychopath thinks. Knowledge is the most powerful weapon you can ever hope to deploy in an attempt to defeat these human predators.

Glossary

Clinical Description: A description used by a psychologist or psychiatrist to objectively describe the characteristics and symptoms of an individual's mental and behavioural disorders.

Depersonalisation: A term that refers to an offender who psychologically views their victim as an object as opposed to an individual human being.

Desensitisation: A process in which an individual becomes used to particular events, thoughts or stimuli through frequent exposure. For example, constant exposure to violent behaviour will minimise an individual's reaction to it.

Deviant Cognitive Coping Style: Refers to an individual's mental inability to cope with situations or process information in a socially normal or acceptable way. Inappropriate or strange behaviours become a part of their coping mechanisms.

Deviant Parental Model: Refers to a parent who models or exhibits strange or inappropriate behaviour in front of their children. For example, a father who rapes the mother in front of their child demonstrates that this is a form of power and maintaining control.

Disorganised Serial Killer: A serial killer that leaves evidence at the scene of the crime through lack of thought and planning. The disorganisation may be caused by mental illness, use of drugs and alcohol during the crime, inexperience of the offender, or a low intellectual capacity.

DSM-IV: Stands for Diagnostic and Statistical Manual of Mental Disorders (Fourth Edition). A classification of mental disorders used by clinicians and researchers.

Dysfunctional: A subjective judgement that refers to something that is not functioning or operating as it should. In relation to psychopaths this term relates to a family or lifestyle that is potentially harmful to an individual's future mental wellbeing.

Hare Psychopathy Checklist: A checklist used by trained clinicians to assess the level of psychopathy exhibited by an individual. A score is compiled based upon the pattern of factors observed.

Homicidal Triad: A pattern of three behaviours commonly observed throughout the childhood of serial rapists or killers. These behaviours are cruelty to animals or other children, a fascination with fire (pyromania) and enuresis (continued bed-wetting after the age of 9–10 years).

Manifest: Refers to the development and/or exhibition of behaviour that relates to the subconscious.

Negative Social Attachment: An individual's feeling or view that they are not a part of or wanted by society. There is also a hatred of or ambivalence toward people within that society.

Organised Serial Killer: A serial killer who has planned and thought carefully about the crime, leaving very little forensic evidence as a result.

Predisposition: A term that refers to a factor that increases the likelihood or susceptibility of an individual to adopt behaviour he/she has been exposed to.

Profile: Personality and behavioural characteristics of an offender deduced from examining the crime scene.

Profiler: A person trained in understanding and identifying the criminal psychology and behaviour of the criminal. Typically, a profiler is a psychologist, psychiatrist or specially trained law enforcement officer.

Serial Arsonist: An individual who lights three or more fires in separate incidents.

Sexual Assault: Defined as any sexual activity carried out against the will of the victim through the use of violence, coercion or intimidation.

Bibliography

Britton, P. 1997, *The Jigsaw Man,* Bantam Press, UK.

Britton, P. 2000, *Picking Up The Pieces,* Bantam Press, UK.

Canter, D. 1995, *Criminal Shadows,* HarperCollins, UK.

Cook, S. 2001, *The Real Cracker,* Channel Four Books, UK.

Douglas, J. & Olshaker, M. 1996, *Mindhunter,* William Heinemann, UK.

– 1997, *Journey Into Darkness,* William Heinemann, UK.

– 1998, *Obsession,* Simon & Schuster, New York.

– 1999, *The Anatomy of Motive,* Simon & Schuster, New York.

Hare (PhD), R. D. 1995, *Without Conscience: The Disturbing World of the Psychopaths Amongst Us,* Simon & Schuster, New York.

Harrower, J. 1998, *Applying Psychology To Crime,* Hodder & Stoughton Educational, UK.

Hazelwood, R. & Burgess, A. W. (eds) 1995, *Practical Aspects of Rape Investigation: A Multidisciplinary Approach* (2nd edn), CRC Press, USA.

Hazelwood, R. & Michaud, S. G. 1999, *The Evil That Men Do:*

FBI Profiler Roy Hazelwood's Journey Into The Minds of Sexual Predators,
St Martin's Press, USA.

Holmes, R. M. & Holmes, S. T. 1996, *Profiling Violent Crimes: An Investigative Tool,* Sage Publications Inc, USA.

Hughes, R. 1986, *The Fatal Shore*, Alfred A. Knopf, New York.

Jackson, J. L. & Bekerian (MRC), D. A. 1997, *Offender Profiling,* John Wiley & Sons, USA.

Keppel, R. D. with Birnes, W. J. 1998, *Signature Killers,* Arrow Books, UK.

Masters, B. 1996, *The Evil That Men Do: From Saints to Serial Killers,* Doubleday, UK.

Norris, J. 1990, *Serial Killers: The Growing Menace,* Arrow Books, UK.

Ressler, R. K., Burgess, A. W. & Douglas, J. 1988, *Sexual Homicide: Patterns & Motives,* Lexington Books, USA.

– 1997, *I Have Lived In The Monster,* Simon & Schuster, UK.

Ressler, R. K. & Shactman, T. 1993, *Whoever Fights Monsters,* Simon & Schuster, USA.

Seltzer, M. 1998, *Serial Killers,* Routledge, New York.

Vorpagel, R. & Harrington, R. 1998, *Profiles In Murder: An FBI Legend Dissects Killers and Their Crimes,* Plenum Publishing Corp, USA.

Wilson, C. 1996, *The Killers Amongst Us: Motives Behind Their Madness,* (two book series) Warner Books, USA.